GET MINDFULNESS RIGHT

Unboxing the Powerful Practice for Mental Well-being

Swati Desai, PhD
&
Subhashini Prasad

Om Books International

First published in 2024 by

Om Books International

Corporate & Editorial Office
A-12, Sector 64, Noida 201 301
Uttar Pradesh, India
Phone: +91 120 477 4100
Email: editorial@ombooks.com
Website: www.ombooksinternational.com

Sales Office
107, Ansari Road, Darya Ganj,
New Delhi 110 002, India
Phone: +91 11 4000 9000
Email: sales@ombooks.com
Website: www.ombooks.com

ISBN: 978-93-5376-977-2

Printed in India

10 9 8 7 6 5 4 3 2 1

To
the teachers in my life
My mother, Vibha
My life partner and biggest support, Bhagwan
My kids Paheli and Saransh
And all my students of mindfulness!
Swati

To
the A-stars in my life
My little life coaches, Arhaan and Aarna
My calming partner, Ayush
My pillars, Amma, Appa and Aravind
for seeing me through the ebbs and flows of mindfulness
Subhashini

Contents

SECTION 6: MINDFULNESS IN REAL LIFE

Preface

In 2021, amidst the thickness of the pandemic, I reached out to Subhashini with an idea of writing a book on mindfulness. As a long-term teacher of secular mindfulness, I felt restless about how it had been misunderstood and underutilised. I had loved Subhashini's earlier writings and reached out to her to collaborate. In addition, her life exemplified a modern stressful life—budding writing career, MBA from a prestigious business school, two young kids and tons of ambition—the type of life the power of mindfulness can be harnessed to manage meaningfully.

I discussed my concerns with her—in the process of popularising secular mindfulness, it got stripped off the important and supportive practices that existed in Buddha's original teachings. I felt that the correct concept of mindfulness must be shared, especially with the Indian audience, many of whom think it is a Western tool and do not realise that it is very much rooted in the Indian soil. In fact, I believed that the Indian mindset is especially primed for using mindfulness to increase mental well-being because of our collective unconscious from centuries, enabling us to have a deeper understanding of concepts such as non-attachment and the sacred. Moreover, the modern Indian cannot find solace from only religious rituals, they need psychological explanations to practise well-being.

The popular version of mindfulness is defined as 'being aware of the present moment'. Though easy and attractive, to reduce stress is only one aspect. There are a lot of other factors that make it into a life-sustaining tool. Mindfulness is a beautiful refuge for finding purpose, focus, equanimity and stress-free pursuit of excellence.

Subhashini was sceptical at first. Like others, she had many doubts about the practice. How could the teachings of the Buddha help anyone in modern times battling personal and societal pressures of *an entirely different kind*? How is learning about the practice of mindfulness different from sitting in meditation with guidelines on an app? Could one do this without years of meditation practice and without having to give up other meaningful practices one has in life?

What she found really intriguing was when I said, 'one crucial outcome of mindfulness is to be able to delay auto-pilot reactions and then take effective action'.

Imagine a superpower that could help us delay (preferably completely avoid) screaming and fighting in an argument. A superpower that helps us reflect on our passion instead of quitting on our dream. A superpower that helps us sit with pain until we find a solution. A superpower that can make us more in control of our happiness.

That is the mindfulness I wanted to write about and make it accessible to everyone—one that can be practised by both a newbie like Subhashini and a seasoned meditator.

As two women from different walks of life, we bring a unique combination of voices to convey mindfulness: Grit and wit. Professor and student. Generation X and millennial. Empty nester and young parent. Expert and subject. Traditional and modern.

I was born and brought up in India and then moved to the US for higher studies. I have lived in two continents. After many years, I returned to India for work and study. I have had two types of careers: technical in maths and computers and then in psychology.

Although my life was full of adventures and unusual experiences, I suffered from some ailments. I was addicted to external validation and admiration. It made me do selfish things and hurt people, exactly the opposite of what I intended. In reality, all I wanted was intimate and positive connections with people.

After many tears and explorations, I found mindfulness. My background from India helped me absorb it on a deeper level. I connected with it because it was not based on any religious rituals or philosophies that required me to surrender to a guru.

My Western education allowed me to appreciate the research-based foundations of mindfulness and its solid foundations in psychology. This was very important to me. A perfect blend of the East and the West, which I diligently wanted to bring into this book.

Today, I am married to a wonderful man for over thirty years and have fulfilling relationships with my kids and extended family. My life has changed because I explored mindfulness in its entirety. Compassion, communication and commitment—the three pillars of good relationships came to me because of mindfulness. I accept the imperfections of life—which are aplenty—but I allow myself to feel them and then watch them mindfully.

I have learnt to take effective actions as opposed to going for instant gratification. I have come a long way and I still have a long way to go. It is a lifelong path. A good reason to write this book as this is what I want for every reader.

Subhashini had her own reasons to co-write this book. Born Indian, raised Indonesian and educated American, her identity has been fluid and challenged time and time again.

In the United States, her ambition to be a successful professional was marred by her pride to be purely Indian. In India, she found happiness in being a working mum until she quit it all to pursue her passion for writing.

Despite being an author of two bestselling books, she was always made to feel she had made the wrong decision of giving up her career and pursue her passion for writing full-time. Additionally, being a full-time mum of young children during the pandemic only seemed to deepen her angst of not knowing where her life was headed.

None of the parenting handbooks and guided meditation videos seemed to help her. Until she started helping me in penning this book, she thought mindfulness was a boring subject reserved for those retired and wanting to attain a monk-like life. But helping me in writing this book has converted her from being a sceptic to a believer, still learning how to implement the theories into practice.

I have been teaching mindfulness as a psychological tool for well-being since 2006 in universities and on my website (2meditate.com). I received formal trainings and certifications in mindfulness and mindful self-compassion in the West and formal training in meditation practice at Mr Goenka's vipassana centres in Hyderabad, Bodh Gaya and Mumbai.

I continued my deep dive into mindfulness as years passed by and also got into studying the early Buddhist teachings in a formal structured programme at the Spirit Rock Meditation Center in California and InsightLA Center in Los Angeles. In this process, I realised how the practice of mindfulness in popular culture there was so inadequate. Its full potential of changing one's life was not fully understood.

India was no different. My professor friend from a prestigious business school once said to me, 'Mindfulness really teaches you to live in the moment. Although that is an important concept for enjoying the moment, how would it help when your loved one passes away? How would it help for a leader to become ethical and caring? It doesn't really help you to handle competition.' This further convinced me that in the process of secularising mindfulness, we may have lost answers to such questions that come from Buddha's teachings. We need to put him back in mindfulness, but in a way that is relevant to our modern life.

It has been my mission to show mindfulness in a comprehensive way. This book shows how to do mindfulness right by sharing true stories of my students, by knowing all the correct principles and by learning the meditation activities to practise it. Having Subhashini as the co-writer has greatly helped express and convey my thoughts and ideas. Her journey with mindfulness warrants to be written in an honest, relatable and, at times, revelatory way.

While I bring in stories from patients, clients and students, Subhashini has written them in a way that is easy to retain. Since she has sincerely practised the mindfulness activities in the book, she has shared them in ways that is worth writing.

The book is divided into six sections. The first five sections explain the concepts, nuances and how to practise each of the four aspects of mindfulness. The concluding section of the book documents mindfulness in real life. There's a chapter on how parents can apply mindfulness when parenting their kids. The final chapter gives specific stories of mindfulness champions who practise it in real life.

After reading each chapter, practise mindfulness in your life, and when you do so you will invariably have questions. Go back to the chapter and you will find the answers. Practise it again. It is only when you understand it right, it will make a difference in the way you conduct your life. Each day you practise, you will find freedom from habitual reactivity that creates distress and find a new wholesome way to experience joy. This is what makes mindfulness a powerful practice for mental well-being.

SECTION 1

Mindfulness—an Introduction

1

Get Mindfulness Right

Debunking Myths about the Timeless Practice

'The First Noble Truth is that there is suffering, *dukkha*. This must be penetrated by first fully comprehending suffering.'

—Buddha

Burn your thoughts

Mr Neil was a hard-working and successful middle-aged professional. But his life was never the same when he lost his only son to a freak car accident one year ago. What was supposed to be a smooth-sailing ride called life had come to a grinding halt.

Mr Neil was almost drowning in guilt and anxiety and was unable to sleep for weeks. Upon the recommendation of his doctor, he came to me to learn mindfulness. His goal was 'to make peace with misfortune' which though hard to achieve was not impossible.

We started our session by drinking a cup of tea *mindfully,* feeling the warmth of the teacup in our hands, observing the rays of sunlight reflecting from its surface and immersing in the gingery aroma of the drink. Mr Neil found it very soothing and admitted to having never enjoyed tea so much.

He agreed that anxiety and vigilance are habits that can be unlearned and he started *paying more attention to the present.* On his nature walks, he was starting to notice leaves, flowers, the colour of the sky and even the chirping of birds.

However, this state did not last long. The real challenge started when he participated in the exercise, Burn your thoughts. Mr Neil was tasked to pay attention to his feelings and thoughts, both positive and negative, and write them all on pieces of paper.

He had to then segregate the pieces of paper into two piles—one pleasant and the other unpleasant. Mr Neil was asked to throw all the pieces of paper with uncomfortable thoughts into the imaginary bonfire in front of him.

'Let them burn!'

'Let them burn!'

I repeated softly as Mr Neil breathed in and out. He seemed viscerally relieved to let go of the unpleasantness.

Then, I asked Mr Neil to do the unthinkable: 'Throw all the pieces of paper with pleasant feelings and memories written on them into the fire as well. Don't cling on to them.'

'Mr Neil started pacing up and down the room, unable to throw his pile into the fire. In a few minutes, he broke into a sweat and knelt down, crying.

'The good memories are all I have left of my son and burning them means that I am letting them go. I want to hold on to these memories and relive them when I miss him. I don't ever want to feel sad and guilty,' he told me hesitantly, wiping his tears.

I was glad he accepted the dilemma he was facing. He was struggling with the present because he was desperately clinging to the good memories of the past, with the hope that he could relive them as soon as any distress showed up in the present. I sat with him and said,

'Almost 80 per cent of the students in my mindfulness classes define it as "present moment awareness" or "living in the moment". But that creates huge limitations for finding long-term contentment.'

'Mindfulness is indeed to develop a present-moment awareness and to notice the beauty of this moment but it is much more than that. If you want to transcend pain and anxiety, please don't skip the reality of the pain. Let it be and observe. Without reacting or seeking escape. Hold yourself kindly while suffering. And when you do that, observe what arises in you.'

Mr Neil hesitated but did not quit. I urged him to experience everything that was coming to him—not only honouring memories and enjoying the present, but also accepting the pain of the guilt and the struggle to reconcile.

Slowly, he crumpled the papers with good memories written on them and threw them into the bonfire and sat still for a long time. He did that for the next few days. One day, it occurred to him that by letting go of the past, he was able to rewrite his story in his mind that made sense to his present situation.

He saw himself as a gentle and good father who was just deeply sad because of a huge loss. As tears rolled down his cheeks, he felt love arising in his heart for himself and his son.

'My son is telling me that I was a good father,' he said. 'This is life! And my son wants me to take life as it comes because that's what he is doing too.'

After a long pause, Mr Neil smiled and told me his son was always a precocious kid and how he used to advise him on what to do. He was able to recall this with a smile on his face. For the first time in over a year, Mr Neil was able to sleep through the night again.

Want to look tiger in the eye? This book shows you how

This book aims to be a handy mindfulness teacher like Mr Neil needed; to provide a comprehensive approach needed to experience all the richness life has to offer.

What is the one thing in common that an astronaut in uncharted space, a working mum of twins with a vibrant social life and a successful do-gooder entrepreneur have? The ability to look a tiger in the eye, stay calm under pressure, make wholesome choices and stay in the moment. And do it all with a sense of purpose and well-being. How do we acquire that?

Although present-moment awareness is indeed a crucial aspect of mindfulness, it is not enough to equip us with this superpower. For that, we need to set on the path of comprehensive mindfulness. What is the point of learning to swim if it does not help us break waves and enjoy swimming in the lakes, rivers and beaches with equal pleasure?

The purpose of this book is to:

- Teach all the comprehensive and rich aspects of mindfulness with all their nuances and intricacies that are missing in the popular understanding and offer a unique one-stop access to everything one would want to know about mindfulness.

- Provide a toolkit to practise each aspect.
- Reinterpret the ancient teachings on mindfulness and apply its each aspect to our modern life problems for increasing our sense of well-being, without having to practise any religious rituals or without giving up any religious practice we may already have.

What is mindfulness?

Some of our readers may be completely new to mindfulness and some may already be practitioners of this technique. Regardless, let me start by presenting its most basic definition. I have carefully coined it using the existing definitions and from our own experience.

Mindfulness is the ability to be aware of whatever you experience in the present moment, with curiosity, with total acceptance, without judgement, without jumping to reactive actions and by simply observing instead of getting carried away by your feelings.

This definition emphasises a very important factor—being aware of the present moment; however, it also encourages us to become *less reactive* and to observe whatever is happening around us without resisting. It creates an important space between our feelings and us immediately expressing them in their raw form, hence giving us a chance to open up our perspective to new facts and also to choose an effective way to act.

This basic definition is only a prelude to something bigger. In the original ancient teachings, mindfulness needs to be learnt with associated trainings and practices. This comprehensive way to learn and practise mindfulness is what helps transform lives by getting insights into difficult emotions, 'impossible' relations and conflicting events, emotions, experiences and what we do with them.

Mr Neil's grief was unfathomable. But his journey to living a guilt-free life and mindfulness would be half-baked if he had focused only on cherishing the present moment. A half-baked journey can result in relapse and being more frustrated than before.

What separates someone who can float in a shallow pool of life from someone who is ready for both the pretty sunsets and high tides?

A comprehensive approach to mindfulness is your answer.

Four crucial factors of mindfulness

Mindfulness needs to be explored along the following lines to live a sane, passionate and meaningful life. The popular understanding of mindfulness is one-factored: awareness of the present moment. The comprehensive approach to mindfulness includes practising the following:

1. present-moment awareness,
2. non-attachment,
3. compassion and
4. core values.

These tools have several nuances that need to be understood beyond their clichéd meanings. Otherwise, they may sound like empty jargon. Only when we start reading, understanding, practising, questioning and reading again, we enjoy the power of the comprehensive framework. Then we enjoy long and non-reactive swims as opposed to interim breathless dips in and out of turbulent pools.

Myths about mindfulness

During the years of teaching mindfulness, I have come across several misconceptions about the practice that the beginners hold which sometimes stops them from exploring it fully. They need to be debunked.

Meditation is the only route to achieve mindfulness

Meditation is the fastest route to make the brain mindful. However, it is *not* the only way. One can practise mindful activities (discussed later in the book) and acquire the ability to be mindful.

Mindfulness is a relaxation technique

Mindfulness allows us to relax and reduce the stress as a by-product of the practice. However, it is much more than a relaxation technique. It gives us insights into the phenomena underlying the problem we are experiencing.

One can achieve mindfulness by taking a course

If we take a pre-recorded course or follow an app, it will familiarise us with mindfulness and its practices. It will certainly put us on a path to learn how to be mindful. Doubts and questions will arise. A book like this is meant to address the most common questions asked by students. You can easily go back to reading a chapter when in doubt and contemplate to find a deeper meaning. Although asking questions to a teacher is the best way to clarify doubts, you will still need a book like this too for remembering the clarifications, augmenting explanations and discovering your own meaning.

Following Buddhism is imperative to achieve mindfulness

Mindfulness is a secular practice. We do not need to know about Buddhism (or Hinduism) to practise it. However, because Buddha's teachings are the source material for mindfulness, going back to it will give a deeper appreciation of the theory and practice.

Mindfulness will make us stoic

Comprehensive mindfulness involves the practice of non-attachment with compassion. They balance each other. Non-attachment teaches us to objectively observe life's realities with our thinking brain but compassion teaches us to open our heart to suffering with kindness and good wishes.

To quote the renowned Buddhist teacher Pema Chodron, 'Loving kindness towards ourselves doesn't mean getting rid of anything. It means we can still be crazy after all these years. We can still be angry after all these years. We can still be timid or jealous or full of feelings of unworthiness. The point is not to try to throw ourselves away and become something better. It's about befriending who we are already.'

Practising mindfulness techniques will curb our passion and ambition

Mindfulness puts us in an objective observation mode. Hence, it may seem as if it curbs mad passion. However, passion is like fire—it can burn you if raging or it can be controlled to help you cook.

We may fall in the trap of assuming that passion and ambition need to be like a raging wildfire but when we practise non-attachment, along with compassion and core values, it will direct our passion into a non-overwhelming and purposeful task. In fact, mindfulness may even be helpful with pursuing our passion because it saves us from getting burnt out.

The ancient practice of mindfulness is impractical in the modern world

Mindfulness is a general-purpose technique that is time-independent and culture-independent in its strict form. It increases the awareness of the problems in an objective way and enables us to look for the most effective solutions for ourselves. Mindfulness is a foundation for managing problems.

We will come up with the best possible solutions for ourselves as mindfulness will give us incredible insights into our problems. Thus, the solutions we come up with will change depending on the time we live in.

Aha! Moment

If I understand the gaping holes in the popular practice of mindfulness and digest the ancient comprehensive version, I can enjoy the whole buffet of life without the stomach ache and visit to the doctor.

2

How McMindfulness Has Entered the Popular Psyche

Minding Past Mistakes

'Those who cannot remember the past are condemned to repeat it.'

—Philosopher and critic George Santayana in *Life of Reason,* 1905

'I understand mindfulness is not about just living in the moment. Maybe it is about being kind, not taking oneself too seriously and knowing who we really are,' I told Swati one day, still perplexed like Po, the Kung Fu panda, in front of his Master Shifu.

Swati asked, 'Is that *all*?'

'Having a sense of humour? And building strong, lifelong relationships? And possibly, resisting the urge to grab a doughnut and ice cream every time I have a problem?' I added cheekily.

Swati laughed and told me I was nearly there.

'Don't you want to have the superpower of an astronaut, a juggler mum and a successful do-gooder entrepreneur?' Swati asked. I nodded vigorously. 'Then let us understand how the *power of now* became the popular understanding of mindfulness and why it is inadequate.'

How mindfulness went mainstream

To truly understand the current understanding of mindfulness, it is important to understand how three modern, remarkable men steered the common man to think of mindfulness as primarily present-moment awareness.

Jon Kabat-Zinn and the mindfulness for stress reduction

> 'The real meditation is how you live your life.'
>
> —Jon Kabat-Zinn

In 1979, Jon Kabat-Zinn was a molecular biologist trained at the Massachusetts Institute of Technology (MIT). For years, he had been practising vipassana[1] meditations (mother of

1 Vipassana is the ancient Buddhist style of meditations translated as 'insight'. Mindfulness is foundational to vipassana. One starts with practising mindfulness meditations with the intention of gaining insights into life's truths, particularly how our experience is always changing and how everything is dependent on several factors, including our sense

mindfulness meditations) at the Insight Meditation Society founded by dedicated Western Buddhists like Joseph Goldstein, Jack Kornfield and Sharon Salzburg. As the folklore goes, one day while sitting in his office, Jon had an epiphany that there was no religion in Buddha's teachings and hence it can be used in medical settings for treating patients suffering from chronic pain. This led him to design an eight-week programme which included secular meditations and movements to help participants to completely accept the pain as it is and to learn to attend to the present moment as opposed to the past regrets or future worries.

The title of this programme was called Mindfulness Based Stress Reduction (MBSR). Many patients who participated in the programme reported that they did not experience the pain in the same way any more after years of medically unresolved issues. Encouraged by the results, Jon offered the programme to another set of people, this time setting up a proper research protocol that eventually led to published papers and the bestseller *Wherever You Go, There You Are: Mindfulness Meditation in Everyday Life*.

> In the case of mindfulness, it is something that has very ancient roots in humanity and is, I would say, universal in its availability to us as human beings. So although it is, formally speaking, the heart of Buddhist meditation practice, it really is universal, as most of Buddha's core teachings have to do with the nature of mind and the

---

of who we are and what belongs to us. This helps to cultivate non-attachment. Burmese Indian teacher Satya Narayana Goenka, known as Guru Goenkaji, popularised vipassana in India starting way back in the seventies. He set up many vipassana retreat centres all over India and later in the other parts of the world.

> nature of reality, and not being part of a particular kind of clique or subset or religious group… I found ways to speak about it that avoided the risk of it being seen as Buddhist, new age, eastern mysticism or just plain flakey.
>
> —Jon Kabat-Zinn, Vox, 19 December 2023

'Mindfulness is "the awareness that emerges through paying attention, on purpose, in the present moment, and non-judgmentally to the unfolding of experience moment by moment.'

—Jon Kabat-Zinn, University at Buffalo website

Over the years, the evidence-based efficacy of MBSR was confirmed in research papers by other scientists. MBSR's reputation grew rapidly as the go-to non-invasive stress reduction programme in the US and Europe and was soon offered in most major medical facilities.

Jon Kabat-Zinn came to be known as the father of the secular mindfulness movement. The success of MBSR and Kabat-Zinn's books spread the word about secular mindfulness, and his emphasis on the non-judgemental awareness of the present moment made mindfulness synonymous with 'living in the moment'.

Although Kabat-Zinn's contributions to popularisation of mindfulness as a secular tool was absolutely seminal, he had taken away Buddha's emphasis on compassion and core values as essential accompanying practices. The word 'non-attachment' was excluded from the MBSR vocabulary, possibly because of its roots in Eastern asceticism. Even today, many mindfulness teachers respectfully find MBSR limited to stress reduction and not about adding enough meaning or depth to life. This book aims to correct this.

Dalai Lama and the science behind mindfulness

'The development of our minds and our destination in future lives is in our hands. No one else can help us. It is very important that we each take responsibility for ourselves. Sustain mindfulness twenty-four hours a day.'—Dalai Lama

In 1979, His Holiness the Dalai Lama, made his first trip to the US. After that trip, he started making rounds of the other Western countries, learning English so that he could communicate the Buddhist teachings to everyone.

Dalai Lama became an international symbol of peace and became immensely instrumental in popularising the 'East meets West' foundation of mindfulness. He encouraged the Western scientists to do what they were good at—use modern research tools to verify claims made by Buddhist teaching on mindfulness and other concepts.

In 1991, he co-founded the Mind and Life Institute in Charlottesville, Virginia, to test the validity of claims from contemplative traditions using scientific methods. He wanted Western science and Eastern wisdom to create an evidence-based wisdom tradition. He encouraged and inspired many neuroscientists to test if the claims of mindfulness as a tool for reducing stress and increasing happiness held up to the rigour of scientific studies.

Richard Davidson from the University of Wisconsin and Sara Lazar from Massachusetts General Hospital were among them. Davidson conducted neuro-imaging studies of the brains of Buddhist monks at the university. He followed them up

> ***'Precisely because of this scientific component, mindfulness is gaining traction with people who might otherwise find mind-body philosophies a tough sell ...'***
>
> ***Time* magazine on its cover story 'The Mindful Revolution', January 2014**

with studying non-meditators' brains before and after training them into an eight-week-long mindfulness training.

Lazar did extensive work at Mass General studying neurobiology of long-term and short-term (eight weeks) mindfulness practitioners after her own positive experience with such practices.

They conducted their own independent studies with electrodes attached to long-term meditators. These studies were designed to test if non-meditators too can experience a similar impact after undergoing short-term training such as MBSR just as long-term meditators who had many years of practice. The astonishing discovery was that the short-term meditation training too resulted in positive changes in the brain although not as intense and as pronounced as long-term meditators. The positive results from mindfulness practice seemed dose dependent: longer the better. They documented that practising mindfulness even after just eight weeks of training resulted in:

- a changed brain structure,
- reduced anxiety,
- better emotional regulation,
- improved perspective taking and compassion, and
- reduced mind-wandering and self-referential thoughts.

Results of these studies not only turned heads, but also captured the imagination of thousands of people who were experiencing symptoms of the twenty-first century disease in a globalised, super-competitive world of extreme stress.

By 2020, many researchers had studied different aspects of mindfulness. Not all of these studies provided robust results. But one thing they did for sure—mindfulness became the most researched tool for psychological well-being. It had gained a reputation for being a non-invasive, secular and evidence-based tool that could give you better control over your happiness level.

Consequently, it spread like wildfire in the corridors of hospitals and psychological counselling centres and filled columns of respected publications such as the *Atlantic* and *Scientific American*. In January 2014, *Time* magazine ran a popular cover story 'Mindful Revolution' discussing in detail how mindfulness resonated with 'America's fast-paced, stressed-out masses'. It even arrived in the boardrooms of corporations and leadership literature in business schools. It was applied to handle eating disorders, anger management and stress-related diseases, and reported success.

Mindfulness had definitely become the tool to try out in all types of situations.

Eckhart Tolle and the 'power of now'—a phenomenon

'Wherever you are be there totally.'— Eckhart Tolle, *The Power of Now: A Guide to Spiritual Enlightenment*

In 1999, Eckhart Tolle published his book *The Power of Now* after suffering from depression for most of his life.

He dropped out of his PhD programme in Cambridge and spent years studying and spiritually guiding fellow students before writing his book, which contained ideas from Buddhism, Hinduism, Mysticism, Christianity and spiritual awakening.

The book advocated that the only way to find true peace and fulfilment is by being solely and intensely present in each moment. The more we live in the now, the more we connect with our true selves and experience life fully.

> ***Eckhart Tolle's influence in the way people thought about spirituality grew so much that in 2011,* Watkins Review *named him one of 100 most spiritually influential living people in the world.***

Oprah Winfrey credited *The Power of Now* with helping her to 'get through 11 September 2001' and she featured it on her December 2002 *Oprah's Favorite Things* show. The book's popularity grew so immensely that by 2008, it had been translated into more than 30 languages and sold three million copies a year later.

Professionals rushed, crazed, tired, stressed, confused, overwhelmed by competition latched on to this simple idea—drive all your attention to the present moment and you will be awakened.

Thus Kobat-Zinn's secular mindfulness and Tolle's power of now made present-moment awareness the most influential and spiritually attractive idea in the realm of mindfulness. Dalai Lama's immense influence piqued the Western scientists' curiosity to test Buddhist ideas in labs and opened the public's mind to trying them out.

However, the underlying principles have been forgotten in popular culture. The aspect of present-moment awareness was easy, attractive, pleasant and useful for relieving the stress of the moment. After all, the current generation is always on the lookout for an easily accessible way to reduce their stress.

Along with it, something strange happened in the Buddhist world. Western Buddhist teachers who had spent years on meditation zafus and in isolation chambers of minimalistic Eastern-style meditation retreats were suddenly in demand. They were delighted to see that their lifelong conviction was finding its well-deserved place in the West.

The Googles and Apples of the world started inviting them to train their employees to be less stressed and more in touch with the present moment.

But something got lost in the way.

McMindfulness: the peculiar mix of spirituality and capitalism

'Anything that offers success in our unjust society without trying to change it is not revolutionary, it just helps people cope.'
Ronald Purser,
Mindfulness: How Mindfulness Became the New Capitalist Spirituality

The ubiquitous use of mindfulness as a tool became confusing and divisive among Buddhist teachers as highlighted by the term McMindfulness, coined by the Buddhist teacher and psychotherapist Miles Neale in 2010. Neal described it as 'a feeding frenzy of spiritual practices that provide immediate nutrition but no long-term sustenance' (http://www.markwk.com/book-notes). Ronald Purser further popularised the term in his bestselling book *Mindfulness: How Mindfulness Became the New Capitalist Spirituality*. He has argued that the branding of mindfulness as spirituality meant that it can be consumed like fast food, helping people to cope but without allowing people to address the root causes of their problems.

The term points to the all-pervasive run-of-the-mill use of mindfulness. Some believed that the purity of mindfulness teachings had been diluted.

Leaving aside the Buddhist context of mindfulness in the quest for secularism is like taking a soft petal from a rose to enjoy its velvety touch and never knowing the beauty, scent and the completeness of the whole flower.

What got lost also was the fact that the Buddhist context around mindfulness too could be as secular as the present-moment awareness.

As the well-known story goes, Prince Siddhartha left his kingdom and became a wanderer looking for solutions to the universal experience of distress and suffering that we all seem to experience, including illness, ageing and death. When he found his answers, he became the 'Buddha'—the enlightened one. His sole goal was to provide practical solutions for reducing suffering and increasing joy. He had no interest in metaphysical discussions on existence of God or a soul, neither did he think of himself as a god-man. He made observations of problematic psychological, cognitive, behavioural tendencies and suggested methods to alter them. In this sense, Buddha was the earliest known cognitive behavioural psychologist. To emphasise, I consider Buddha to be a psychologist and not a religious leader, and often refer to him as Dr Buddha in my sessions.

Buddha came up with a list of things one should do to get out of this pit of dread we fall into and the addiction to the pleasant experience we crave obsessively. Their rightful place in mindfulness practice has unfortunately been lost.

Why the 'present-moment awareness' is limiting?

The present-moment awareness factor of the mindfulness practice creates a huge limitation in the way it is practised.

This makes people crave only the pleasant experience of smelling the roses. This *addiction* to getting rid of unpleasantness can create a denial of life's realities which eventually show up. It also pushes aside the reality of modern life—you need to remember lessons from the past and plan for the future.

We cannot bypass the pain if you want to grow into a stronger, hardier and better person. We cannot bypass the slightly deepening sea levels or a high tide while learning to swim in the sea. Mindfulness teaches us how to *stay* with a painful experience until the reality behind the pain becomes clear.

This book will help you use the three boosters to present-moment awareness—non-attachment, core values and compassion—to lead a content and fulfilling life and reap all of the benefits like the ones described below.

CREST: the mountain top of benefits

Concentration: Ability to focus on any task at hand paying little heed to distractions.

Relaxation: Reduction in stress, anxiety and depressive feelings.

Equanimity: Evenness of the mind and dealing with the ups and downs of life better.

Self-awareness: Becoming aware of one's mental patterns and hence one's full potential.

Taming: Taming self-sabotaging habits that arise from ways to escape pain.

Each benefit has the potential to show up as positive results in our daily life. They can be linked to the four aspects of comprehensive mindfulness.

Benefit	What results you can see	The aspect of mindfulness that aids the benefit
Concentration	Improved productivity	Present-moment awareness
Relaxation	Improved protection from stress-related diseases and chronic pain, better sleep patterns	Present-moment awareness, non-attachment, compassion
Equanimity	Stronger relationships	Non-attachment, compassion
Self-awareness	Effective decision-making	Present-moment awareness, non-attachment, core values
Taming	Enhanced lifestyle	Present-moment awareness, non-attachment

Source: Authors

Aha! Moment

I can get CREST of mindfulness by understanding the foundational principles from Buddha's original teachings. Without that, it becomes simply a tool for momentary enjoyment.

Come, walk through life on these four, steady legs with ease.

3

Mindfulness Mapped to Its Ancient Roots

Relieving the Brain from the 'Baggage of Evolution'

'The most important factor in survival is neither intelligence nor strength but adaptability.'

—Charles Darwin

What a scientist and a sailor teach us about life

A scientist and a mariner met on a ship. Strangers meeting by chance, the grey-haired scientist looked at the young sailor with envy. With a drink in his hand, the scientist taunted the sailor.

'Young man, do you know how this ship was built?'

The sailor shook his head in denial.

'Do you at least know how humans learnt to go from a wooden raft to building a cruise ship?'

Slightly embarrassed, the sailor said, 'No, I don't.'

The scientist laughed mockingly at the mariner and got up to leave his company when they both heard a deafening thud. Passengers were running away from the ship's deck into their cabins. Terrified, the scientist and the sailor looked at each other and took cover. A circuit had exploded and the ship was about to sink.

The sailor tapped the scientist's shoulder and asked, 'Do you know how to swim?'

The scientist nervously shook his head and whispered, 'No.'

The sailor grabbed the scientist's hand and as they jumped out of the ship, into a canoe, the sailor anchored it in a safe spot and smiled.

'Did the knowledge of the ship's construction save you or did my knowledge of swimming and sailing?'

To derive the benefits of mindfulness and transform your life, we do not need to know how it was constructed; however, our brain works better with context. When we know the origins and the context, our understanding deepens and our experience becomes richer. Hence, this chapter on the origin of mindfulness.

Satipatthana Sutta: Buddha's original teachings on mindfulness

The first ever detailed description of mindfulness can be traced back to Buddha's discourse called Satipatthana Sutta. *Sutta* in Pali means discourse and *satipatthana* could be translated as establishing mindfulness. This is part of a huge three-volume compilation of Buddha's teachings, called *Tripitaka,* written in mid-1st century BC in modern-day Sri Lanka around four hundred years after his death. It summarises Buddha's teachings as recalled by his disciples.

Satipatthana Sutta is a step-by-step guide to four types of mindfulness meditations—a unique style of meditation in which we neither empty our minds of thoughts nor fill it with any God's image or a mantra. In each type of meditation, we are instructed to pay attention to some aspect of our experience of the present moment.

Here is how the sutta introduces why we should practise these mindfulness meditations.

'*Ekāyano ayam, bhikkhave, maggo sattānam visuddhiyā, sokaparidevānām samatikkamāya, dukkhadomanassānam atthangamāya, ñāyassa adhigamāya, nibbānassa sacchikiriyāya, yadidam cattāro satipatthānā.*'

'Mendicants, the four kinds of mindfulness meditation are the path to convergence. They are in order to purify sentient beings, to get past sorrow and crying, to make an end of pain and sadness, to discover the system and to realise extinguishment.'

What four?

The sutta then goes on to describe four meditations and how to practise these as indicated below:

- Contemplate your body (*kaya* in Pali) diligently, ardently, clearly knowing, constantly letting go of the greed and distress concerning the world.
- Contemplate your feelings (*vedana* in Pali) diligently, ardently, clearly knowing, constantly letting go of the greed and distress concerning the world.
- Contemplate your thoughts and mental patterns (*chitta* in Pali) diligently, ardently, clearly knowing, constantly

letting go of the greed and distress concerning the world.

- Contemplate your values and the right ways to do things (*dhamma* in Pali) diligently, ardently, clearly knowing, constantly letting go of the greed and distress concerning the world.

The rest of the sutta then describes the details of the four meditations. For example, 'contemplate your body' consists of details such as breath, posture, situational awareness and so on. In the same way, details of the other meditations are given.

How are the four meditations related to the four facets of mindfulness?

When we meditate like this, we are ardently focusing on what is happening to our body and mind in the moment; this cultivates the present-moment awareness. This awareness helps us notice how our mind works, how it creates stories, how it affects our body, and how our thoughts and feelings are so fleeting. We can save ourselves a lot of angst by learning to observe the reality of our mind and body as opposed to getting sucked into the delusions our mind creates. This helps us reduce clinging which means increased non-attachment. The fourth meditation is about contemplating dhammas—the core values. We notice what values create meaning for us. This is an important step towards finding wholesome joy in life even when practising core values could be difficult in the moment. The diligent observation of reality puts us in touch with the pain that all human lives hold. This, along with the contemplation of core values, gives rise to the wish to help others. This is what compassion is about—understanding suffering of others and wishing to help.

Stories our brain creates ...

No one dares dispute your story once your brain has created it. There is no difference between a person who is hallucinating and you! Our brain mixes up facts with non-factual interpretations. Consider these examples:

The hallucinations of an A+ student

Until my A+ student-daughter finished her undergraduate degree, she used to routinely feel that she was going to fail the exam in the difficult maths class she was taking that quarter. If I reminded her of her stellar record in other maths classes, she would say that this time it was different.

Fact: She was overwhelmed by the workload.

Interpretation: She was certainly going to fail the class.

The dilemma of a stoic colleague

Monali's colleague did not smile at her one day in the corridor and did not even acknowledge her in the meeting. Monali thought to herself, *he does not like me*. Of course, it makes sense because Monali disagreed with him in the last meeting and he seemed unhappy.

'If you judge after appearances, you will continue to be enslaved by the evidence of your senses.'

Neville Goddard, *Gratitude Journal*

Monali then concludes that he does not like disagreements. Interestingly, Monali does not consider the possibility that her colleague forgot his glasses that day and did not notice her!

Fact: Colleague did not smile.

Interpretation (*in Monali's mind*): He does not like me.

The fight over a small misunderstanding

Our friend took his girlfriend to meet his mother for the first time. She seemed anxious and distressed during the whole car ride. He interpreted her anxiety as her apprehension to meet his mother. He became anxious himself and a bit disappointed. The girlfriend denied his claim that her anxiety was because of the apprehension to meet his mother.

She said her promotion was going to be decided that weekend and hence she was preoccupied. Our friend did not believe it. He held on to his belief. The car ride turned out to be stressful for them both.

Fact: She was anxious and preoccupied about her promotion.

Interpretation (in the friend's mind): She does not love me enough to want to meet my mother.

Taj Mahal in our imagination

As a middle school kid, I remember being intrigued by a poem in my local language Marathi titled 'Taj Mahal in My Imagination'. The poet describes how the Taj Mahal in his imagination is probably so unbelievably beautiful that he has decided never to visit the real Taj Mahal ever! The real one will never match the one in his imagination.

Haven't we all had this experience of dreaming and making scenarios in our minds of the good things we anticipate? It could be a date, a vacation, a promotion, an award for you or your children or a piece of chocolate you are craving.

Occasionally, expectations do match the reality. However, they are still short-lived. When the charm starts waning, we either grieve or latch our imagination on to the next desire. When we long for something, we are making great enchanting stories of how good we are going to feel once we get it. Taj Mahal as a man-made wonder is a fact and everything else is an interpretation.

In short, we are often hallucinating. Buddha called them delusions. When we cultivate mindfulness, we begin to recognise our own stories and patterns as delusions, thus sparing us a lot of distress.

We are also saved from such impractical thinking, which can lead to disappointments. The objective brain we develop by practising this would not take any craving or aversion too seriously and as a result, would be called a *non-attached* brain. We would be leading more honest and tolerant lives. We may even be happier.

This is a good enough reason for wanting to reprogramme our minds to respond to the modern life's concerns. Our life changes so rapidly that it helps not to be attached to today's interpretation of feeling or thought or sensation too seriously.

But wait, there is more! When our brain starts buzzing with interpretations made after we get feelings and thoughts, we quickly act upon these as if they are facts.

My daughter who was afraid of failing the class would experience stress and anxiety and suffer an upset stomach. She would not be able to focus as well on studying for the upcoming exam, which only aggravated her fears.

If we interpret that our colleague does not like us, we will not smile openly when we see them the next time. We may agonise over our colleague spreading rumours about us and as a pre-emptive strike, we may slight the colleague.

When we experience the drama of getting angry with someone close to us, we create a whole war with the person by either yelling at them or ghosting them out completely. Once our anger subsides, we may realise that our actions were melodramatic at best and a relationship killer at the worst.

We suffer the consequences of taking feelings and thoughts very seriously without being mindful of the fact that they are impermanent and often unreliable sources of fact-based information. Buddha's mindfulness training is asking us to consciously monitor this by:

- Collecting different perspectives—simply observe and ensure that we have all the facts and then decide what the effective action is going to be.
- Employing the wisdom of *non-reactivity*— the ability to not act on feelings and thoughts right away. Wait and see.
- Non-attaching from intense cravings and aversions.

But what if the delusions are indeed facts?

What if the colleague who did not smile indeed does not like us? What if we found out about the unflattering words our colleague used to describe us? What if the A+ student fails in a class because that semester's anxiety was unbearable? What if we get angry at a person who truly tried to dominate us by pointing fingers at our shortcomings?

What if we do not want to be dominated and felt good about giving it back by yelling at the person? What if we decide to buy a fancy car as a signal of our worth to our community and it does get us more friends and more social acceptance? In other words, all stories made by our brain may not be hallucinations. They may indeed be facts.

Fear not because facets of mindfulness offer various choices for handling reality.

How to use the four aspects of mindfulness to handle reality

Cultivate compassion for ourselves and others when we need to reconcile to a seemingly unfair fact of life, such as anxiety or disapproval from colleagues or loved ones or unfairly not getting the promotion we deserve.

'Freedom is the space between our feelings arising and us acting.'
Viktor E. Frankl

Train ourselves to stop impulsive reactions and observe objectively, that is, with non-reactivity or non-attachment; and reconcile to the difficult aspects of our own behaviour. For example, we may find that when we feel self-righteous anger towards a person, we are completely hijacked by our un-empathic side and it typically does not result in convincing the other person why we are feeling such a wrath.

Remind ourselves of our own core values and check if we are violating them. Core values are the guiding principles in our life which tell us what would feel 'right' for us. For example, if your core value is emotional self-sufficiency, you may not always follow parental advice even when it is difficult. Or if your core value is right livelihood, you will not do anything unethical or harmful to make money.

But before deciding what the right effective action is, *we need to stop our automatic, instantaneous reaction and learn to react in a desirable way*. Simply observing and non-reactivity in the present moment are the ability to not act out immediately and potentially, regrettably. We need to train ourselves to tolerate the discomfort in the present moment. When we non-attach from the intense cravings and aversions in the moment, we end up saving a lot of misery.

Will practising mindfulness make us extinct in the long run?

If all this makes sense for making us suffer less, why don't we just automatically do it? Why do we need to *train* ourselves? For that, we need to understand the famous works of Charles Darwin on the science of evolution.

Cultivating an objective, non-attached, non-reactive, value-based and mindful brain is going against the programming of evolution, the hardware of the brain wiring. The driving force in the Darwinian theories on how species have evolved by using natural selection is the drive to survive and spread our genes. To do that, we need to watch out for dangers lurking around in our surroundings. As the book *Sapiens* describing the history of humanitys explains: 'We are constantly imagining things that could be hiding around the corners, a uniquely Homo sapiens ability, even when we do not see it or smell it or have no sensual awareness of it.'

Evolution does not care if the story our brain is making up is correct or the mental turbulence it can create is unpleasant. It only cares about keeping us alive by creating a flight or fight response in our sympathetic nervous system.

It also creates the pull towards a desirable object by creating all kinds of imaginary pleasures, which seem to wane once we get the object of our desire. Evolution wants us to eat as many sweet fruits right now because we need the dose of energy from sugar. Ancient man did not know when the next meal was coming.

As per the law of diminishing marginal utility, we all know of the story where a farmer ate ten apples and with each apple, the taste became less appetising and hence undesirable. Even then, the next time the farmer was hungry, he was delighted to discover the ten apples and grabbed them all.

So, to follow Buddha's advice means to swim against the stream of evolutionary pull towards intense cravings that keep us alive enough to pass on our genes. It is also against the intense aversions that make us jump at every threat we perceive.

Evolution is less concerned about how robustly happy and harmonious our lives have become and more about how we react to stress and adversity. *If so, will cultivating mindfulness make us less distressed but dead sooner*? Will we lose our flight or fight response and survival instincts? How do we reconcile and make sense of Buddha's advice and Darwin's observations on our survival needs?

How cultivating mindfulness is critical for survival in the modern age

The answer to this dilemma lies in knowing basic findings from evolutionary biology and evolutionary psychology.

The field of evolutionary biology and evolutionary psychology agrees that our culture and civilisation have been advancing at an enormous pace over decades but biological evolution works slowly over millennia. Our brain's response by 'natural selection' is not going to match the way we have set up systems around us.

We are stuck with our prehistoric brain-at-birth struggling to function in the twenty-first century. The evolution of the brain to suit the environment is an exceedingly prolonged process.

The classic case of a sabre-toothed tiger charging at us and we deciding on the spot whether to fight or to run away is no longer the fact of everyday life. We do not fear going out of the house driving or walking as a life-and-death event.

Today, we have already tried to change the common evolution-based forces by creating birth control, antibiotics and vaccines, economic and physical infrastructure to take care of the weak and by creating paid services such as insurance so that we can avoid social dependence on each other for survival.

What we fear most in today's world are feelings arising from stories cooked up by our brain, which believes that it is trying to save our life. The brain is unfortunately stuck with the 'baggage of evolution'. The sabre-toothed tiger that we worry about today is entirely different from the prehistoric times. Today, the threats we face are different:

- Finding and sustaining work that can allow us to pay our loans and educate our kids.
- Responding to the intense need to fulfil our material ambition and to survive the immense stress that comes with it.
- Managing relationships, break-ups, monogamy and expectations from partner equality.
- Seeking approval from others and wanting to be understood and nurtured, but this is at odds with everybody being too busy in their own lives.

- Needing to be emotionally and financially self-sufficient and yet, requiring human connections.
- Caring about others without losing ourselves.
- Figuring out how to manipulate interacting with people from different cultures and with diverse views.
- Making sense of the new social movements and the conflicts they may create in our minds.
- Managing the information overload and the lack of trust in its authenticity.

Since we are stuck with using ancient hardware to tackle modern-day problems, we need to use our brain's software by writing a new code to create neuronal connections that can respond to contemporary problems more effectively.

We need to change our inherited and ingrained habits into more adaptive ones. How do we change our habits? Is there a method? Buddha's teachings on mindfulness give us a method to change old habits and to create awareness and insights into an effective way of taking care of the new problems.

It is to cultivate an objective, non-attached, non-reactive, value-based and mindful brain by following the instructions in Satipatthana Sutta in its entirety.

The survival of the fittest must include mental health, increasingly so since our brain is so ill-equipped to tackle the problems of modern life. The mind and body connection implies that our level of calmness is instrumental in creating that in the body as well.

Studies from the field of positive psychology show that cultivating compassion and values that generate positive feelings has the potential to improve our immune system and our personal resources through social connectedness. Evolutionary psychology proposes that compassion and altruism are traits that have helped us survive better as a group in which we stand united.

Aha! Moment

My brain's 'stories' were useful for my early ancestors to physically survive in the savannahs and forests, but in today's world these stories may be destroying my mental health. So, my survival will benefit from mindfully watching out for reality and intentionally training in positive habits like showing compassion and following other core values!

With this motivation to rewire our brain's software, let us start understanding and practising comprehensive mindfulness.

SECTION 2

Present-Moment Awareness

4

How to Practise Living in the Moment

Avoiding CRASH And Burn

'Practice does not make perfect. Imperfect makes us practice.'

—Mokokoma Mokhonoana

The year 2020 was a difficult one for everyone. Into the thickness of the pandemic, there was a week when everything went wrong. Subhashini's parents were admitted in the hospital for Corona, her husband lost his uncle and she had not slept all night with two sick kids at home.

So, when after another tired day of cleaning and cooking, she saw that her children had drawn on the wall, she lost it and screamed at them. The look on their scared faces still disturbs her. When I spoke to Subhashini, she recollected thinking she knew it all; after reading several parenting handbooks, following mindful parenting handles on social media and occasionally meditating.

It was not until she started understanding the nitty-gritty of mindfulness that she realised learning things in theory will be useful only if implemented and practised. One cannot learn driving by reading a book; mindfulness is like that. Whatever benefits you know mindfulness can bring you, practice cannot be skipped.

Practice makes you aware of your imperfections before you choose to change them. Comfortably. With ease. Reading the driving manual is important to know the rules but ultimately, the real test is when you can drive to a grocery shop without having to think about each gear.

Mindfulness meditations

Meditation is an act of focusing on a pre-decided entity and gradually allowing our system to settle into doing just that by turning away from everything else that comes in our attention span.

There are many different types of meditations: transcendental meditation is when we focus on a mantra. Heartfulness meditation is when we focus on our heart's sensations. Some meditations focus on a god's image or a candle. In another type of meditation, we are expected to empty our mind of thoughts in order to have a thoughtless, blank mind.

In mindfulness meditation, we focus on some aspect of our experience of the moment. We learn to objectively watch the experience to know the reality of the moment. We can choose to focus on the experience of breath, body, feelings and thoughts in that moment. We learn to observe it with curiosity, with total acceptance, without judgement and without reaction. Simply observing. When we formally sit and do not do anything else but just this, it is mindfulness meditation.

In this chapter, we will suggest three mindfulness meditations and five activities. It helps to do at least one of them as part of our daily routine.

Meditation 1: get to know your breath for five minutes

In this meditation, we pay attention to our breath in the present moment. This is difficult because our attention wanders. But we learn to bring it back to observing our breath. We also learn to pay attention to the sensations that arise when we breathe in and out. We need training to learn to pay attention to subtle sensations. This meditation allows us that training. This is really to prime into a deeper experience of the subsequent meditations.

Meditation 1: Get to Know Your Breath

Sit in a calm place without distractions, with your back straight.

1. *Notice the sensations:* With each breath in and out, notice how it is received by the body. By noticing how the little nostrils are feeling the sensations. Maybe the lungs and the tummy feeling the sensations. Open up the attention with curiosity.
2. *Observe:* Let the breath follow its normal pace. No need to change it. If you happen to breathe shallow, you notice that it was shallow. No need to correct it right away by breathing long. Just watch and practise non-reactivity. Even when it may seem boring, continue to do it for the time you have decided.

3. *Wandering attention:* If your attention starts wandering, simply bring it back without guilt.
4. *Practise non-judgemental attention:* Notice the judgements your mind makes but don't take them to heart. If the breath brings us any association, worry or maybe simple boredom, try not to get sucked into it by stopping the meditation. Instead, learn to simply observe: *This is how boredom feels like at the moment. Aha! Let me go back to watching my breath.* See for how long you can sustain the attention.

As you will see, this is not going to be easy. Many obstacles will come in the way of focusing. Your job is to keep removing them all the time when you are trying to be mindful.

CRASH: common impediments while meditating

While meditating, we experience some commonly experienced impediments, which are known as CRASH.

Craving Comfort

While meditating, we will feel physical or emotional discomfort. It is tempting to want to quit and seek a position of comfort.

Remedy: It is okay to do gentle readjustment if the discomfort becomes distracting. However, do not quit. In a way, you are training your body to sit through the discomfort. The mind and body are connected. Hence in regular life, this type of meditation practice gives you the ability to sit through emotional discomfort and still continue with your plans.

Restlessness

As you sit down to mediate, anxious thoughts can arise, for example, about pending tasks in hand, which can make you restless, wanting to complete the task at hand instead of sitting still and silent.

Remedy: One way to reduce restlessness is to choose a time of day when you have least distractions to do your meditation practice. Start with two minutes of meditation practice and gradually extend it to five minutes or more. If you still feel restless, say to yourself, 'I am restless at the moment' or 'This is anxiety' or 'Let me see if I can sit through this during the time I have decided'. Another thing that works well is to meditate with someone else. The accountability can keep us going in spite of restlessness.

Aversion

We may experience aversion to the idea of meditating because of physical discomfort, boredom or strong feelings of hatred or anger directed at someone.

Remedy: Observe the aversion. Urge yourself to continue. For physical discomfort, two strategies work: (i) paying objective, non-reactive attention to the pain in the body and see it as pain, and (ii) moving away from the pain and paying attention to the part of the body or mind that feels comfortable.

Sleep

A very common experience is to start falling asleep during meditation or at the end of it.

Remedy: Try opening your eyes or even standing up for a minute to let go of the drowsiness. Become aware of how the sensation of sleeping feels like in the body.

Hesitation

It is only natural to start doubting the process. Doubts about its benefits or if you are doing it right start popping up. If the expected benefits are not materialising, meditating seems pointless.

Remedy: It helps to know that having doubts is just a phase in any path. Spiritual masters say to stick to a path for ten years before you decide to change it. Sometimes, you need to struggle with doubts and clarify them by reading, discussing and thinking. Sometimes, you may want to switch to contemplating over the doubts in the meditation itself.

Activity 1: telephone challenge

Although we blame technology for creating distractions and reducing our attention span, we can use it for planning a mindful activity. When our phone rings or pings with a notification and when we reach out to pick up the phone, we need to STOP!

Stop.

Take a deep breath.

Observe the energy coming in body.

Proceed.

First STOP and then pick up the phone. This will take only a few seconds. If we do it twice or three times in a day, it changes our awareness of a deep breath and challenges our association with technology. Most importantly, this cultivates the habit to become aware of the moment.

Tantrum Tina

Tina was a sensitive and an emotional child. The smallest of anomalies would irk her. She would scream at an imperfectly cut sandwich or swear at being denied a fourth piece of chocolate. Her mother, utilising her own journey with mindfulness, used to advise Tina to 'take a deep breath', every time she would want to scream or cry. However, Tina never followed the advice.

She grew up as an anxious person and hence decided to learn mindfulness, among other things, determined to manage her anxiety. When she took my classes, she took the telephone challenge seriously. First, it was mechanical. She did it only because she liked the idea of accomplishing the homework.

Then one day, when she felt anxious, she paused and took a deep breath. What she felt was different; she felt a surge of energy through her body. Her body instantly relaxed. It felt like things would be fine. She told herself that her anxious feeling will pass too.

Tina reported to me, 'I felt the power of attending to the breath, the most fundamental and glorious phenomenon that keeps us alive.'

An initially mechanical activity had taught her how to use the breath as a necessary pause, a reminder that everything can be okay!

Meditation 2: get to know your body

Now that we have primed our attention to focus and notice the breath sensations that we typically don't notice, let us use this skill to get closer to a very fundamental and universal part of our existence—our body. Body is the ultimate seat of our experience. It was Buddha who made us realise that all our emotions and experiences are ultimately felt in the body and that is what we respond to.

If we feel pleasant bodily sensations in response to a feeling, we would want to experience that again and again. For example, if feeling angry creates pleasant feelings in our body as a reaction to an event, we would seek ways to be angrier. (Yes, anger feels good in the body and mind for people who see a benefit of control in it.) This information can help us in changing our anger-seeking behaviour if we understand that it is destroying our relationships. So, knowing our body and trying to change the sensations in it are ways to slowly gain control over our reactions.

Meditation 2: Get to Know Your Body

Sit in a calm place without distractions, with your back straight. Start meditating for two minutes and go up to 20 minutes. Then, more! Before starting, decide the duration of the meditation and then sit for that long even if you feel tempted to stop.

1. *Do a body scan*: Start at the top of your head and slowly allow the attention to slide down sequentially through every part of your body. Allow the attention to stay in that part until you notice some sensation on the skin and under it. See if you can simply observe what that sensation brings to you as an observer and not as a participant because feelings may get triggered. The important part is to only observe and not react.
2. *Check if your mind and body are interacting:* Feelings and thoughts may come up and may show up as body sensations. Or body sensations may make your mind think, interpret and feel. If there is an unpleasant sensation in the body, can you tolerate it? Can you still continue sitting and meditating even when tears may fall down your cheeks?

3. *Cultivate equanimity:* See if you can accept your bodily sensations without getting entangled in the sensations—craving them if they are pleasant or hating them if they are unpleasant. Attempt no judgements. See if it is possible to observe the whole experience like this. By doing this, you are cultivating equanimity.

Activity 2: pause, notice, savour

When we are going through a good moment, we often let it pass. We enjoy it in retrospect or when we look at pictures. We may have taken a beautiful nature walk or serendipitously connected with someone in a party or had a lovely time with the family or received a great news in the mail we were waiting for over the whole summer! More often than not, we enjoy it but not fully.

We suggest to **p**ause, **n**otice and **s**avour (PNS). Here and now. At the peak of the moment and not as an afterthought. At the moment when your child takes her first step and not when you watch the video later. At the moment your spouse smiled at you on a crowded bus and not later when you mention it to your best friend.

Guess where we want to turn our attention to? To our body. How does this moment reflect in the body? Warmth in the tummy? Tingling in the hands? Relaxation in the back? A feeling of a full heart? Giddy in the head? Goosebumps?

Such PNS moments have another advantage. The parasympathetic nervous system is activated when we enjoy and focus on our happy moments. If we practice PNS moments, we are also training our parasympathetic nervous system to kick in.

After practising it with good moments, we can use this training even in the middle of a stressful moment. Pause, notice, *allow* the body to relax and mindfully acknowledge that there is more to life than fighting the cause of our stress.

Activity 3: mindful tea drinking

Pick a drink of your choice. Let us say your morning cup of tea. Just for a few sips, pay attention to your five senses slowly and with curiosity. How does the tea look, smell; the touch of the cup; the sound when you are slurping and then the taste. Pay attention to whatever comes through these five senses. Experience each sensation. Savour each moment.

If the tea is cold, do not jump to heat it up or add more sugar if the sweetness is not to your liking. The activity is to ensure not to fall for the shortcomings of the tea. Experience the fullness—good and bad—with equal acceptance and non-reactivity.

In the process, a sixth sense can arise. You may have feelings and thoughts because of associations and memories getting triggered as you drink the tea. Just notice and observe them without stopping the drinking and without acting upon any of the feelings. Believe it or not, this is great training for life situations.

Sometimes, we need to carry on with the experience without getting distracted or without falling for the judgements that may arise.

Activity 4: mindful of an activity

During the day, there are several parts to our routine that require our body. Taking a shower and walking from one place to the other. We may do gardening or cooking. Choose any such activity in which you can observe your body sensations and the feelings and thoughts that arise. For a minute or two, do just that, similar to how you experienced tea drinking. No changing anything, just fully living it by using awareness.

Students ask if they could choose to implement this exercise while watching a movie or reading. The answer is 'not really' because one can easily get absorbed in a movie or in a book. Getting absorbed would in fact (counter-intuitively) be the opposite of being mindful. One could be lost in the story or be watching the movie keenly. It would be hard to be aware of our body sensations when we are lost in the story.

Saved by mindfulness

A fellow mindfulness teacher used to work with veterans who were experiencing post-traumatic stress disorder (PTSD) after war. Sometimes, the symptoms would remove them from reality and make them believe that they were surrounded by danger. The teacher worked with the veterans over a long period of time to be aware of the body sensations and not to act upon them immediately.

One night, the teacher got a call from one veteran, D'Souza. He said he knew it was late at night but he had to report something urgent. D'Souza was having a hard time with his hallucinations. He had an urge to run out because he felt a sense of intense fear. Rushing out would have meant running into the middle of the road, unaware of the vehicles and traffic lights. But he recognised his body sensations before he acted out on that urge.

With practice, he had learnt to observe the sensations and relax his body. He stopped himself from desperately running out into the traffic. After a few weeks, the urge subsided. D'Souza was immensely grateful to be alive. Hence, the call to the teacher.

The body awareness meditation training had given D'Souza the ability to recognise and control his distortion of reality.

Meditation 3: awareness of feelings and thoughts

Our mind is typically full of thoughts and feelings. Once we recognise the drama that our brain makes, we can have some control over navigating our reactions. When we are dealing with unpleasant feelings and thoughts, it helps to know that the experience does not represent the whole of us. It is only one part of our life and personality. We can remind ourselves that stories made by our brain may not represent reality. We need to wait and see what new information becomes available. All this can be summarised in the following way in meditation: *Not me, not mine, not the whole of me*.

Meditation 3: Awareness of Feelings And Thoughts

Sit in a calm place without distractions and with your back straight.

1. *Label your feeling(s)*: Sit formally and delve deep into your mind to check the feelings. Are you feeling excited, calm, joyous, anxious or agitated? Recognise what feeling(s) is (are) arising in that moment. Label it and tell yourself, 'I am feeling anxious.' Recognise the most prominent feeling showing up in your mind.
2. *Attend to your thoughts:* These refer to sentences, explanations, musings, analyses or comments that form in your mind. If you pay attention, you will notice them crowding your mind. Simply observe and accept whatever is arising without any judgement. Only recognise with curiosity what exists.

3. *Notice your bodily sensations:* Notice how these feelings and thoughts are being expressed in the body. Any aches, pains, temperature change, pressure, butterflies in the stomach, tingling sensation? Our previous priming into noticing body sensations is very useful.

For some, it takes time to know how feelings are being expressed in the body. Some can be over-vigilant and interpret each body sensation with alarm. Both traits need to be moderated for accurately knowing what each body sensation means.

4. *Observe the experience:* Ultimately, what matters is whether the experience in your body is pleasant, unpleasant or neutral. This will help you categorise how your body feels, without reacting or judging. Anxiety makes us feel unpleasant, love makes us feel pleasant and doing chores may be neither pleasant nor unpleasant (for many!). Tolerate the unpleasant in the body as practised in the previous meditation.

5. *Repeat this mantra:* Now comes the most important step. Keep this mantra in mind: Not me, not mine, not the whole of me!

If you need to stop this meditation before you reach a place of solace, continue again when you get a chance.

Aha! Moment

This is how my experience of the moment goes:
World <=> Five bodily senses (tangible) <=> Feelings and thoughts
(intangible and not the whole truth)

When I keep reminding myself that my feelings and thoughts do not represent my whole reality and it is not worth basing my whole self-image on them, I take away their undeserved power over my moods. I choose not to get as affected by them.

Activity 5: sounds and body

Wherever you are sitting, close your eyes and start listening to the sounds around you. You could be sitting in a noisy or a quiet environment, in a waiting room, on a plane or in a park.

There are sounds in your surroundings. Notice those.

Sounds may trigger memories. Notice those.

Sounds may generate feelings in you. Notice those.

The feelings can create body sensations. Notice those.

From sounds to associations/memories to feelings to the body.

Notice this chain of reactions. The more you do it, the more familiar you will be with feelings and their manifestation in your body.

The cheating boyfriend

Saloni was a student in my class. When she learnt about how the brain is constantly trying to make logical stories based on what we know, she began to pay attention to her own mental patterns. One day, she finished work earlier than expected. And decided to hang out with her boyfriend.

She called him a few times but he did not answer the phone. The first thought that came to her mind was that he was cheating on her. Since she had had a bad experience in her previous relationship, she became suspicious. Although her current boyfriend had never given her a reason to mistrust him, she was always on her toes. This time, she decided to watch the drama being played in her mind.

Not me, not mine, not the whole of me!

She thought to herself, *the insecure part of me is only one side of me. I also have a strong and rational side. Let me wait and see where this goes.*

Also, she knew that she did not own her boyfriend's life.

It is not mine. Although I wish I could dictate everything he does, she concluded.

In the end, when she got hold of her boyfriend, she avoided acting on her urge to yell at him and mistrust his explanation. She just asked him what had happened. He said he had fallen asleep and he did sound groggy. When he learnt that she was wishing to hang out with him, he was disappointed that he had fallen asleep. It would have been great to have pizza and watch Netflix. This turned out to be a pleasant conversation between the two of them. They could express their feelings openly without overreacting.

From havoc to harmony

At the end of reading through all these exercises, if you are still doubting the process and questioning how the mindfulness practice will impact your life, I don't blame you. Subhashini was just like you, believing that we should go on with our life and just do tasks no matter how we react or how certain situations make us feel.

I want to share what she realised after noticing that she was on the wrong path. Constantly reacting to toddler tantrums or career decisions instead of pausing and being aware of how to proceed motivated her to practise mindfulness the right way.

Over to you Subhashini.

In the process of writing this book, I started doing the mindfulness exercises especially the telephone challenge and the meditations to get to know my breath and body. The effects were not immediate but I noticed many changes over a week of practice:

Reduction in doom scrolling: Taking a deep breath before looking at my phone has significantly reduced doom scrolling. I used to spend three and a half hours on social media per day, jumping from one meme, reel or news article to another. This not only took away time from important things, but also left me feeling inadequate about my life as my brain was making up stories of how others' lives look so much better than mine on social media. One deep breath has allowed me to centre this thought process and pay attention to only fulfilling my tasks on social media like doing live interviews and collaborations and gathering the information I need. I now spend two hours a day on social media and would like to reduce it further to be effective.

Understanding my body's cues: Getting to know my breath before getting to know my body really helped me. Knowing your breath first primes you for knowing your body. Having two children under the age of five and letting go of a successful career to pursue writing can result in days of extreme frustration and mum-guilt. The meditations have helped me recognise how my body reacts to certain situations—my jaws tighten first and I feel a light pounding in my head. While this would usually result in me screaming at my kids or gorging on a doughnut or giving up writing for a few days, now it has resulted in plain awareness. I am aware that my body is tensing up and I can move away from the heat of the situation and return to deal with a mess made by my toddler or a publisher rejection. Please note this does not mean I do not have days where I lose it, because I do. But the intensity is far lesser.

Delaying reaction: Delaying reaction is the optimum outcome of mindfulness for me. Because an impulsive reaction is never optimal. Practising these exercises has provided a gap between my body's cues and my reactions. It has helped me feel less agitated about the long waiting time at a bus stop or escaping to binge eat or watch Netflix when faced with a stressful situation. Again, I still do react suboptimally because I am human but my only ask is to be kind to yourself if you do find yourself in these situations and believe that the more you practise, the less you will react.

Subhashini's experience with practising mindfulness is proof that tiny steps towards awareness can have major, sustainable impacts. Keeping up the practice will allow you to reap the benefits further.

SECTION 3
Non-Attachment

5

Understanding Non-Attachment in Modern Mindfulness Practice

A Complete Engagement with Life

'The one who plants trees knowing that he will never sit in its shade, has at least begun to understand the meaning of life.'

—Rabindranath Tagore

The story of a job-hopper

It was July 2020. Ram was barely twenty-two years old.

He was my very close friend's son. Ram had graduated from college worried about getting any job since the Covid lockdowns had dried up the market. However, he had a good academic record which helped him acquire a corporate job as an associate with an upward trajectory. Although this job was not his first choice, Ram was happy to have a well-paying one.

However, he found himself unhappy very soon. He felt like he was just a pay cheque—always expected to meet a challenging target and not treated like an individual who had his own expectations, issues and creative needs. He quit in a few months and took up another job at a small start-up, expecting that it would allow him bigger responsibility and more personalised treatment. This was during the work-from-home phase of the Covid pandemic.

Ram was happy with the new job profile because he felt like he was contributing directly to the growth of the business. But things changed quickly. After two months, he started having problems because the only interaction he had was with his boss who was extremely tough and critical. He had no social interaction with his colleagues, which allowed him no outlet for his frustrations. This was not what he wanted in life. This job too was no fun. He felt stuck, frustrated, scared about the future, anxious, wanting to quit again.

His family was unhappy with this job-hopping. My friend, Kiran, was extremely worried about him and asked me if I could suggest anything that would help her son. I wanted to talk to her first because her anxiety and anger at Ram's career choices were not helping anyone. I asked her what she was so attached to. Was it an image of what her son's successful career should look like? Or how his bad career choices would reflect on the family, especially his upbringing? She grudgingly admitted that this was one aspect.

I told her that if her primary concern was that her son should have a good life, she needs to leave him alone to figure out his own journey. It would help if she does not act out her worry on autopilot by giving him passionate (and mostly incorrect and unsolicited) advice because she could not bear her own pain. She could learn to live with it and let Ram live with his own.

She agreed. I taught her a couple of meditations to help her practise not acting out and staying non-attached. She learnt to not react even when she saw Ram struggling and learnt to be there to listen to him as if he was a close friend's son and not her own.

This was difficult initially, but she soon saw the results! The big step was to reduce her attachment to how 'her family's rèsumè' should look like to the world. She saw that her calmness was helping Ram talk to her more often and, in fact, ask her for some guidance.

I had suggested that Ram take an eight-week-long mindfulness programme to help him ease his anxiety and help him make some choices. Meanwhile, he had quit the job and had decided to take some time off. After many weeks of feeling low and occasionally distracting himself by meeting friends and going to parties, he enrolled in a mindfulness class.

A year passed by when Ram came to meet me to share his thoughts on how that class had helped him and how he had continued meeting a group once a week to keep up the practice. He had taken up a new job a couple of months ago in a more creative environment, with less pay but a more fulfilling role. He said something interesting, 'I have made a commitment that I am not going to quit this job for one year no matter what, even if I start disliking it. I know I can do it,' he said.

'What makes you so confident this time that you can stick around even if things get tough?' I asked.

'In my class, during the exercises and mindful activities, I became keenly aware that I was not equipped to handle negative experiences—especially negative feedback. I was so successful in college that I almost felt entitled that I should always get praised for my work and be given concessions for the time I had some excuses. But I don't have such an unrealistic self-image now. I know that if I stick with a negative experience, it is going to teach me something new. A new awareness. The negativity doesn't stick forever anyway. You know the mantra "this too shall pass". That helps a lot,' he said with a smile.

'What do you do when you feel anxious?'

He smiled again and said, 'I have trained myself to breathe in and out deeply and mindfully, reminding myself of all the good things in my life and taking it in. I also remind myself of my "commitment", which helps me switch gears.'

He continued, 'You know how effusive I am of everything I feel. To escape my insecure feelings, I used to express everything to everybody and seek excitement by going to parties. Because of the mindfulness practice, I learnt that I don't have to spurt them out like before. I practise to let my feelings be and choose whom to tell and what to tell. One other thing! Partying is just a relaxation technique for me. I don't crave it to escape reality any more.'

He added, 'It is not perfect. But that is okay because I feel like I have the tools now. It really helps me to keep reminding myself of the tools because of my weekly mindfulness group.'

What Ram was practising is a powerful tool called non-attachment. While he thought non-attachment was for 'oldies and gurus', this is how I defined it to him:

- Non-attachment is the ability to not cling.
- Not crave for pleasant experiences or run away ASAP from the bad ones.
- Not seek excitement and fun at any cost or intensely hate with all our might.

Simply wanting is normal. What gets us into trouble is the clinging. Because it is like the crazy glue that spills on our fingers and will not go away. We feel miserable until we get the object of our desire or get rid of the pain. We can do all kinds of acts, including self-destruction, to get what we want.

Non-attachment would mean that we desire something without getting caught in automatically acting out of habit. It is about learning non-reactivity.

Non-attachment is when we are able to calmly reflect upon our desires and choose to act the way we believe is effective (which may include passionately expressing feelings). We are able to let go when we find ourselves entangled in a web of misery.

Aha! Moment!

Non-attachment does not mean renouncing all things material, including feelings. It means not being afraid of discomfort. It means full engagement. Because I accept things the way they come without fighting. And I also know when to courageously work on changing them.

My conversation continued for a while. Ram is still at the same job, mostly enjoying and learning a lot. He seems so much more focused on whatever he is doing. Of course, he has a happier mother (and father) now. I would say that this family is more contented because both Ram and Kiran are practising non-attachment for 'feeling good and proud' and to experience 'how things should be' as opposed to how they are. Even when the restlessness returns, they tend not to react right away, not too fast and too much.

During the course of the therapy, Ram raised a few pertinent questions about non-attachment. I get similar questions from others too because the word non-attachment has got some bad rep in modern thinking. Let me clear the misconceptions surrounding it before sharing how to be non-attached.

Misconceptions about non-attachment

Q: Is non-attachment about not wanting any material things?

A: Wanting material things (or anything for that matter) is fine. But does it make you miserable when you are wanting it and not getting it? Does it make you do things that do not fit into your own set of values to acquire the materialistic gains? Is not having it making you lose your sleep and reducing your self-worth? Is the wanting motivated by social comparison?

If the honest answer to these questions is 'No', you are non-attached to material things for all practical purposes.

Q: Practising non-attachment sounds like I am not supposed to have any desire. But desire gives motivation and hope. Giving it up is not always good.

A: Desire can indeed be a motivating and meaningful factor in life. There is no reason to give it up. Practising non-attachment *does not* mean giving up desire. It means *not* clinging desperately to the desire that makes you miserable. The trick is to know how to *let go* of the desperation and still keep the motivation to love life.

Q: Am I going to be detached from everything? From my family? From the people I love?

A: Yes—you may want a solitary house in the hills with no network. On a serious note, detachment is different from non-attachment. Detachment is to stop caring about anyone's well-being. Non-attachment, on the other hand, is caring in a non-clingy way. It will lead to being securely attached to the people you love. Interestingly, to the surprise of many students, it also means not anxiously worrying for the people you love. This kind of attachment is not helpful. It means learning not to impose your solutions on other people because you care about them. As mentioned in the Bhagavad Gita, non-attachment is not when you own nothing. It is when nothing owns you.

Q: With non-attachment, will I lose passion and the zest for life?

A: The short answer to this question is that it is possible and *easier* to pursue your passion with the armour of non-attachment when you experience failure. You will need to navigate skilfully when applying non-attachment to your passion. More about this later in the book.

Q: I like it that non-attachment will reduce my painful feelings, but will I stop feeling the highs too? For example, the extreme pleasure I feel when I accomplish something or when my future spouse accepts or when I have my kids.

A: A valid concern. The highs will be of different types when we practise non-attachment. Non-attachment also means not to cling to a grandiose self-image. This means that when you experience joy, you don't say 'I am so great' but are content with the outcome and understand that success is impermanent.

Q: It all sounds good but how do you cultivate non-attachment? Is there a method?

A: Science and practice show that you can cultivate non-attachment. One established method to cultivate it is to develop a mindfulness practice. We will get to the specifics later in the book.

My personal journey

Psychological or spiritual journeys follow a winding road. Mine was no different. As you read my story, check where you stand on this journey using whatever path you are choosing.

First came enchantment

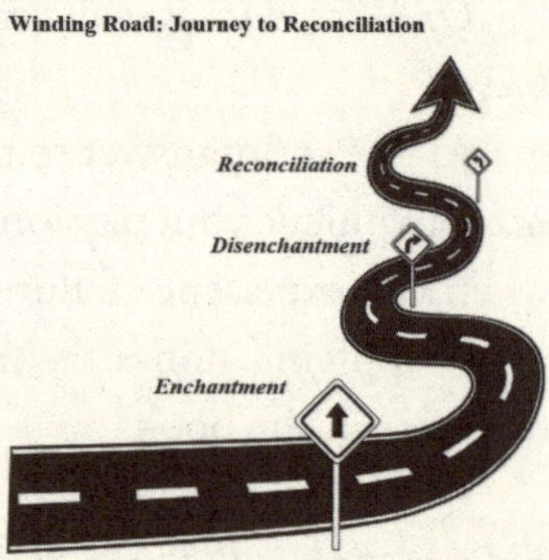

Source: Subhashini Prasad

It all began in middle school and high school in India. I blindly fell in love with non-attachment and the associated philosophy. To most Indians, non-attachment meant an anti-materialistic view of the world with an aspiration towards total renunciation when you reach your old age. In 1970s India, when I was growing up, the notion of non-attachment was central to the popularly known aspects of Indian philosophical systems. I had always thought of non-attachment as a Hindu concept propagated by the Bhagavad Gita and I was not familiar with its central place in Buddha's teachings.

The concept of non-attachment had existed before Buddha but he had made it into his central tenet, expanded on it profoundly and developed a practical method for cultivating it. I was also unaware that many scholars believed that the Gita was an addendum to the Mahabharata compiled way after Buddha's death and that it was greatly influenced by his teachings on non-attachment, well-established in that period.

I was happy to enter competitions to recite the Gita in purest Sanskrit and read out the translation in the process. The most well-known verse from the Gita is:

कर्मण्येवाधिकारस्ते मा फलेषु कदाचन।
मा कर्मफलहेतुर्भूर्मा ते सङ्गोऽस्त्वकर्मणि ।।४७।।

This is translated as:

You have a right to perform your prescribed duty but you are not entitled to the fruits of action. Never consider yourself to be the cause of the results of your activities and never be attached to not doing your duty.—Bhagavad Gita, Chapter 2, Verse 47

As a young and idealistic high-school girl, I was so enamoured by this interpretation of non-attachment from the Gita that I used to study for my exams by sitting on the floor cross-legged since being a student was my duty and I did not want to get attached to the comforts of sitting on a chair with cushions. I did not want to be attached to the 'fruits' of my hard work in the form of 'good grades'. This helped keep my exam anxiety down. It taught me to be calm under the pressures of exams in a highly competitive environment. The process of studying itself was enough to give me satisfaction—although typically, it did yield good results.

I was completely enchanted by 'non-attachment' to the fruit (the result) and focused on my duties as a good student and a good daughter.

Then came disenchantment

My childhood fascination with the Gita was followed by a disenchantment phase after I enrolled as a graduate student at the UCLA in the 1980s to become a computer professional. I immersed myself in the Western educational system. It felt like a privilege to be able to study there, securing a teaching assistant post. India of those days was not global, not on its way to prosperity through capitalistic ideas, but more fatalistic and more prone to karmic explanations. I started looking at the ancient Indian teachings through the eyes of someone impressed with the prosperity in the West—what seemed to have an orderly and disciplined public life with people having a strong belief in their ideas and their ability to pursue them.

In contrast, India was struggling with inter-community clashes and poverty. I went on to interpret the Indian philosophical tradition as anti-progress, anti-ambition, anti-individualism, anti-passion because it encouraged working hard only because it is our duty and not because we want to get the material reward. I started feeling uncomfortable with the idea of simply doing my duty in life. It seemed so passive!

Non-attachment is the reason why India as a country fell behind in the global competition, I concluded rather prematurely. The karmic theory that explained every misfortune is what kept Indians from taking any action to materialistically improve their lot or to fight for their rights. I could not have been more incorrect.

I completely rebelled against 'duty' and 'non-attachment'.

The reconciliation phase

Then came a time in my life when I had to reinterpret the meaning of 'duty'. I had led my life as a free bird, which became unsustainable. Life had brought its temptations that had taken me away from my path a few times. Sometimes, it posed challenges that I had not imagined and was entirely unprepared for, such as a failed marriage during my teen years and, much later, challenges of motherhood in my second marriage. I had a tendency to get good at something and then get disenchanted by it. I would then run away from that endeavour and find something else that was more tempting and desirable. I did not have the patience to stick to my chosen endeavour and to dive deeply into the struggles of mastering it. I was attached to easy validations.

I switched continents, life partners, career paths and my goals in life. Of course, some aspects of these explorations were enchanting. Although I am tempted to say that I am still a free bird and it all turned out to be good, I am also aware of the suffering it brought me and sometimes to the people whom I cared about. Suffering that only led to more suffering instead of bringing more strength. The suffering in 'vain'.

Reconciliation with the Gita

Eventually, I realised what duty as described in the Gita truly meant. Duty is a translation of dharma in Sanskrit, which can also be translated as life's purpose. There are some innate inclinations or capabilities each one of us has and aligning our careers to these gives us a sense of mastery and joy. It is challenging but following it gives us a sense of well-being and fulfilment. This innate inclination has its roots in our nature—something we are born with. Depending on nurture, this capability is manifested into a concrete capability. Our duty is to respond to our calling by letting go of the attachment to 'what looks good' to the world around us.

For example, by nature, I am a caregiver. By nurture, eventually, I ended up choosing psychology and spirituality as my profession. Practising this gives my heart a sense of solace, so much more than the external validations and financial rewards I got as a computer professional. I am following my dharma. By nature and nurture, I feel responsible for my family and once I accepted that as my dharma, my struggles to balance my career and my sense of adventures with my family calmed down. I needed to be the anchor while my family was still young.

My attachment to other things turned into something to observe and not cling to. Also, just like in the Gita, expecting the fruits of this labour from my kids 'becoming' something I wanted was the other attachment to let go of. That attachment was unfair and would lead to suffering in vain.

The millennials and the Gen Z who question duty can relate to honouring their dharma—skills and passions they are inclined to. Not because of the family they are born into but because each one of us has a special inclination we are born with. If we are fortunate, our environment helps to foster it too. Non-attachment to temptations helps to keep the focus and immerse into our dharma. That is when we flourish. I realised that understanding the power of non-attachment would help India prosper without being decadent.

Reconciliation through Buddha's teachings

During my first vipassana retreat, I learnt what Buddha said when he became enlightened and found the way out of the inevitable suffering or discontent everyone goes through. Guru Goenkaji has often quoted Buddha in his discourses, 'House of misery is built by bricks of attachment. You take away the attachment and the house of misery will collapse!'

"House of misery is built by bricks of attachment. You take away attachment and the house of misery will collapse.'
Buddha

How did Buddha define attachment? His definition was simple and in its simplicity lies the genius. We want more of anything that is pleasant. We want to push away anything that is unpleasant. When this want becomes desperate, it is attachment.

After that retreat, I became fascinated with the overlap between the Buddhist teachings and the Western psychology. When I reread the book by psychiatrist and Buddhist practitioner Dr Mark Epstein, *Thoughts without Thinker: Psychotherapy from a Buddhist Perspective*, I understood the two factors discussed in Buddhism that create the foundation for understanding and practising non-attachment.

First, everything is impermanent, and we need to come to terms with 'this too shall pass'. Second, whatever we believe in is tainted by the context in which we view it. The stories our brains make depend on our perceptions. So, we better keep examining them instead of getting caught into defending our self-image. None of the worldly phenomena stands alone as an independent entity.

An extreme example of non-attachment is, say someone has an accident and loses a leg. To be able to view this from the lens of non-attachment helps handle the extreme loss with resilience. Although the absence of the leg may be permanent, the disabled person may rebuild their life. Their identity changes based on what happens after the accident.

Barbie 'shero': the Manasi Joshi story

Manasi Joshi lost her leg in a horrific road accident but found her calling—and international recognition—on the badminton court. Manasi was only twenty-three years old when a truck smashed into her, crushing her left leg which later had to be amputated. Fitted with a prosthetic leg three months after the accident, she returned to the court to pursue her passion.

'It has been a journey about learning and accepting different things. Working hard on things that looked hard but are the new normal now. I used more of my mind (in my game). Made people run, made sure wherever I put the shuttle they end up giving it to my hand so that I could finish the point.'

Manasi Joshi, former world champion in para badminton, France 24, 28 October 2020

Five months after putting on her artificial limb, Manasi won her first gold in an office tournament against able-bodied players. This inspired her to train harder and in 2019, she won the singles gold at para-badminton world championships! *Time* magazine featured Manasi on the cover of their Asia edition and Mattel Inc. celebrated her achievements on the International Day of Girl Child 2020 with a Barbie modelled on her. Manasi Joshi is the second Indian woman—and the first para-athlete to have a Barbie doll modelled after her.

Manasi's story beautifully explains the two factors that go into non-attachment. Firstly, it explains how things are always changing, for example, Manasi's physical and emotional identity. She went from being a badminton champion to a disabled person to being a para-badminton champion. Secondly, the identity depends on who is viewing the status—*Time* magazine featuring a story or her caregiver watching her daily hardships or the days when she may have felt like a victim.

The Barbie doll modelled after Manasi is not a fixed representation of her. Some may find it inspiring and some may find it a marketing gimmick. Given all these facts, one would take neither the pain of being disabled nor the glory of being an icon as permanent or as a sign of greatness. The aim is to not cling to either the pain or the glory but to follow the purpose of our being. That is what makes life meaningful.

Buddha on me, mine or my ideas

There is a saying attributed to Buddha: 'Our erroneous clinging to preservation of a sense of *self* as a permanent and important entity is the cause of suffering.' In other words, we cling to the following aspects of ourselves: 'me, mine and my ideas'.

When we are feeling unhappy, it is imperative to check which one of these aspects is causing the unhappiness. This gives us a good rubric on what we need to come to terms with or 'let go of'.

These aspects of the self can be viewed as three circles that create our own perception of self. As an individual, my thoughts and views make up *my ideas,* the smallest and usually the easiest aspect of the self to let go.

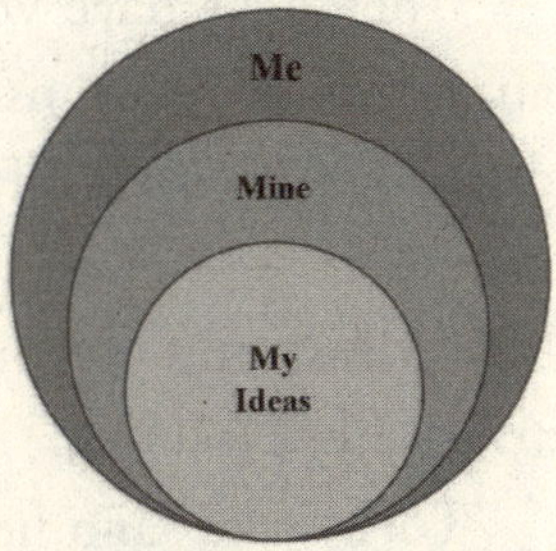

Source: Subhashini Prasad

Mine refers to our physical and emotional possessions like a car, a lucky T-shirt or our life partner. This is the second largest circle of our being and is the one we get attached to easily.

Me is the largest of the circles and refers to a comprehensive image we have of ourselves and is closely tied with how others perceive us: one that is fragile and yet, not easy to change. This is the hardest part to let go and non-attach from.

As one practises non-attachment, these circles that are so tightly knit can drift apart and after many years of practice may ideally disappear altogether. What this means is a sense of fluidity with who you are and who you perceive yourself to be. This fluidity comes from practising non-attachment and questioning 'me, mine and my ideas'.

My ideas: how it affects relationships

Jodie Comer, the actress from the popular TV show *Killing Eve*, is known for her support for LGBTQ+ and Black Lives Matter movements. When she was rumoured to be dating a Trump supporter, the social media platforms started trending with #JodieComerIsOver hashtag. Supporters of liberal causes were asking to 'cancel her' (*The Guardian*, 15 July 2020).

Therapists have written about how difficult it is to have an intimate relationship between a couple who have very different 'my ideas'. It goes against the sense of the self. The way to make it work would be to take away the clinging to 'my ideas' and negotiate the different implications of the attachment to ideas.

Let's take another similar example. Finance Minister Nirmala Sitharaman is married to Parakala Prabhakar. While Nirmala leaned towards the BJP, Prabhakar is from a Congress family. In 2019, he was reported to have openly criticised the central government for the economic slowdown and poor implementation of GST, urging the government to implement a Rao–Singh economic outlook. When political views can be so opposing, how can one overcome attachment to one's ideology in order to maintain a healthy relationship?

Mine: what money can buy ...

Then comes 'mine'. Lack of money and material is a big reason why people experience anxiety. Recent research from Wharton School suggests that people's sense of emotional well-being increases as income goes up and there is no limit at which it plateaues. But the researcher Killingworth warns that money should not be seen as the only means to happiness. While money offers us freedom and autonomy, it is fleeting and feeds into hubristic pride of ownership. Not recognising this can only lead to misery.

Another reason why 'mine' brings us misery is social comparison. Comparing what is mine to what the neighbour or someone close has is a big source of unhappiness for humans. It is imperative to come to terms with the fact that 'mine' brings only a fleeting sense of happiness.

Me: mirror, mirror, on the wall ...

Finally, the toughest phenomenon to conquer is 'me: my self-image' and the way the world views 'me'. After all, we are social animals, we have a need to belong and we want to socially connect with people. Hence, we have a good reason to choose how we want the world to see us. However, when we let it take over without awareness, it can play havoc.

'There is no end to rejecting your body and spending a lifetime doing that. But what really happens is not your body's fault, your body needs at least one person on its side and I said to myself that this is my body and I love it! I've realized it's not people judging you but rather how you judge yourself!'

Vidya Balan (interview with the *Times of India*, 12 June 2021)

Take the example of body image. Appearing stylish and looking slim have become an obsession in today's world. Unless we have that 'look', it is hard to feel confident and good about ourselves. This can create emotional turmoil for many people. While the discourse on body positivity has recently gained traction, it can also be misleading if one gives in to the wrong notion of equating obesity to being healthy.

We are desperate to prove our value to others. Even when we express our vulnerability to people, we are looking for external validation to make us feel better about 'me' or us.

Non-attachment will help us be aware of the factors that made us miserable in the first place. Instead of pushing them away, we will come to terms with them and do whatever we need to make things better. First is to accept them and then we will know what action we want to take.

The 'how' of coming to terms with factors that cause misery is explained in the next chapter.

Hakuin Ekaku—the epitome of non-attachment

A Buddhist monk named Hakuin Ekaku was highly revered and had many devotees in a small village in Japan. One of his followers was a family that owned a food store near Hakuin. They had a teenage daughter who had recently reported to them that she was pregnant. Furious, the parents demanded she revealed who the father was. After much harassment, the daughter revealed that Hakuin was the father of her baby.

In great angst, the parents went to Hakuin.

'Is that so?' he said, in reaction to the accusation.

When the baby was born, Hakuin took him away to raise him. Hakuin had lost his reputation but was undeterred and took care of the child like his own and even brought him milk through *takuhatsu* (alms). A year later, the girl confessed to her parents that the real father of her son was a man who worked in the fish market.

The parents went to Hakuin to ask forgiveness and pleaded to have their grandson back. Hakuin smiled and willingly yielded the child, saying, 'Is that so? It's good to hear this child has his father.'

Hakuin's story is the epitome of non-attachment. He was completely unattached to the idea of me, mine or my ideas. Almost like soap washing off the body during a bath, people's opinion, his pride and ideologies all just slipped off his being. He was perhaps more concerned about protecting the teenage mother's well-being.

You may think that such non-attachment is impossible to achieve, I am totally with you. The example of Hakuin is surely an extreme, but can help us reflect and notice such personas around us. Maybe that successful actor who is resilient to all the media gossip about him? Maybe the teacher in class who never misses working overtime in spite of no additional pay? Being Hakuin is not the goal. But taking the next step towards non-attachment and breaking the tightly bound circles is.

Attachment styles as defined in the West

In Western psychology, attachment to the caregiver while growing up is studied and discussed extensively. Having secure attachment is deemed as positive for later-life success especially in relationships. Attachment, as a result, has a good connotation, unlike in Buddha's teaching which says it is the brick in the house of misery.

My fascination with psychology eventually resulted in my obtaining a Master's degree in clinical social work and establishing my clinical psychotherapy practice. My study of Western psychology familiarised me with the Attachment theory initiated by the developmental psychologists John Bowlby and Mary Ainsworth, in their seminal work on differing attachment styles, in the mid-twentieth century. Their research and the work that followed, especially by Mary Main, shows how the attachment patterns an infant develops for their primary caregiver can influence their success later in life.

In summary, an infant can develop four different attachment styles based on their relationship with their primary caregiver: secure, anxious-avoidant, anxious-resistant and disorganised.

Securely attached

A securely attached infant actively seeks attention from their caregiver and may become distressed upon the caregiver's departure but can be consoled and can reunite with the caregiver with ease.

Anxious-avoidant

An anxious-avoidant infant does not show distress at the caregiver's departure as if they don't care. But when reunited with the caregiver, the infant avoids the caregiver. They seem to exhibit detachment as a defence against their anxiety.

Anxious-resistant

An infant with an anxious-resistant attachment style is uncomfortable exploring strange environments, is significantly distressed when the caregiver leaves, and when reunited with the caregiver is torn between a desire for proximity and resistance to comfort. They may get angry and more difficult to control.

Disorganised attachment

The infant with a disorganised attachment style behaves in an erratic way. When the caregiver returns, they may freeze, run away or show some odd behaviours.

As an infant grows to become an adult, the attachment styles tend to get exhibited in their intimate relationships. For example, the anxious-avoidant style may reflect a distant and unavailable behaviour as opposed to anxious-resistant one that would appear needy and desperate. A disorganised attachment style is typically a sign of childhood abuse in which the intimacy could trigger defence based on the child's situation.

Secure attachment leads to being comfortable with intimacy and healthier relationships and hence is deemed as the most positive attachment style. When the partner is unavailable, securely attached adults can manage the initial distress and let go in time. When the desired partner is available, they can enjoy intimacy with trust. They can explore life without extreme anxiety and trepidation especially when it comes to intimate relationships.

> ***'Non-attachment allows complete engagement in life but with an understanding of life's ups and downs, without acting constantly wounded with hurt pride, with the wisdom to know when to withdraw.'***
>
> **Harvey Aronson, 2004**

Non-attachment can be alternatively looked at as secure attachment in our relationship with life. All other attachment styles have the negative effects of 'attachment' as defined by Buddha or in the Gita. Clinging to self-image, objects, ideas and people can result in either desperately seeking destructive emotionality (resistant) or defensive detachment (avoidant) or a mixture of both (disorganised).

The interpretation of non-attachment as secure attachment in relationship with life is more modern:

- It rejects the traditional religious view of non-attachment as a renunciation of worldly goods.
- It rejects the idea of non-attachment as detachment, which is indifference to emotions and any passionate pursuit.
- It allows complete engagement in life with added understanding that pleasure and pain are all impermanent.

Just like it helps in a relationship to let go of pride and 'me, mine and my ideas', non-attachment benefits from letting go of the need to be perfect and the need to preserve self-image. With secure attachment, a child would neither throw a tantrum nor become a victim. Secure attachment allows us to neither become distrustful of everything nor drown ourselves in social comparison. Action is therefore only taken after accepting the initial distress that the 'mother' is gone and with the trust that the mother always comes back.

Aha! Moment

Non-attachment to pleasures of life is like a child's secure attachment to the mum. What that means is this: when Mum is gone, I cry for some time and then soon start playing with other kids. When Mum returns, I hug her and enjoy being with her. I don't push her away or ignore her because of the anxiety and anger that she had left me. I don't throw tantrums when she is about to leave. I know 'Mum always comes back'.

How to attain non-attachment in mindfulness

If non-attachment is so powerful in bringing us focus, staying on the path, not falling apart from failures, making us resilient, allowing more secure and healthy relationships, how can we cultivate it? Is there a method we can follow to practise non-attachment and delay our reactions?

Yes. There is a method. Buddha was able to formulate one to help us slowly reduce our instantaneous reactions induced by attachment.

The method is to practise mindfulness meditations and mindfulness activities by incorporating them in our daily life. As discussed already, mindfulness practice allows us to implement non-reactivity in our daily affairs. It helps us to stop and then change our autopilot, habitual reactions to things. Watch and observe with a distance. Allow a skilful action to come to mind before implementing it. Non-reactivity is the essence of non-attachment, followed by patience and control. In the subsequent chapter, we suggest specific mindfulness meditations and activities to cultivate non-attachment.

6

How to Cultivate Non-Attachment

Coming to Terms with Pain in Life

'Everything is created twice, first in the mind and then in reality.'

— Robin Sharma, *The Monk Who Sold His Ferrari*

How I got my 'pet' back and made peace with losing her again

It was the summer of 2018. My family and I were all enjoying the holidays and little travels. I own a beautiful blue tea kettle which I used every day to store my morning ginger tea. My family drank that tea the whole day long. I loved this kettle which had weathered my daily use with a lot of scratches. I had used Krazy Glue to put her broken lid back together.

One day, after I returned from a weekend long outing, I just could not find my kettle. I asked the two people who had visited my house in my absence if my kettle broke under their supervision. Both had no idea what happened to the kettle. I searched in all cabinets, all rooms and even in my yard. No sign of my beloved tea kettle! I was seriously missing my tea kettle and all her unusual features.

My mind was creating all sorts of stories. I had some painters coming to my house the day I had returned from my outing. That evening, I had noticed the absence of my kettle. As delusional as the mind gets, I wondered if the painters had taken her. Nothing else but a beautiful broken tea kettle, I chuckled. Then I remembered that I had left my front door open for almost five hours for the paint to dry. *Did someone come into my house and run away with the kettle? Was it a friend of mine who was trying to play a prank on me?* I remembered a similar prank my relative had played on me when I was a high-school girl. The thoughts went on and on.

Fortunately, after some restless time, I chose to simply observe this drama without letting it hijack my peace of mind. Otherwise, it would have nagged me to annoyance. I was amused to notice that my non-attachment training was helping me observe with amusement and curiosity as to where this story was going to go.

Two days went by. I opened the fridge to get a tall bottle of juice out from the top shelf where I stored tall items. And there she was! My tea kettle. Standing tall. I suddenly remembered putting her there, as I was about to leave the house for the weekend, thinking that the tea in the kettle can still be used as iced tea. I had never done this before. I am not an iced tea sort of a person. It was just that my son who loved iced tea was going to visit right after the weekend. I was quite excited to get my little pet back. I was going to enjoy her presence even more, mindfully, from then onwards, knowing that I may lose it again. This is the joy of non-attachment.

Buddha's laws on non-attachment

If a seemingly lost tea kettle can create havoc in our mind, what about the bigger things in life that we cling to? What kind of exhaustion do we put our brains through if it acts delusional all the time? Therefore, we need to cultivate non-attachment. But how do we become non-attached to the difficult experiences and yet, enjoy the moment?

Buddha had two specific laws to explain non-attachment. If we understand and deeply come to terms with these, we begin to become non-attached and our experience of the world around us starts changing. Practising mindfulness meditations and activities helps to imbibe these laws and cultivate non-attachment.

Law of Impermanence

All phenomena and the objects we experience are impermanent. Our bodies, senses, feelings, thoughts, perceptions, habits and patterns change. So do the objects we experience around us, as things age, break, and sometimes our perception of the article changes. There is one joy that comes out of this law. Whenever we experience pleasant feelings, we learn to cherish them because we know they will not last forever. Whenever something painful or distressing is going on, we know 'this too shall pass'. This creates a refuge where we can think clearly even when some pain may still linger on. Understanding impermanence also puts us in touch with what or whom we love. Coming to terms with it suggests that we must express our love *now* instead of regretting not appreciating the person and the object after we lose them.

My kettle's disappearance was a stark reminder of impermanence. One day she will be no more and because of that realisation, I enjoy her in a special way every time I use her.

Exercise

Click your fingers and with every click, say: 'past, past …' Even a click of a finger, which lasts only a millisecond, never lasts and becomes past instantly. It shows that nothing is permanent and all you have to observe is the present moment and not cling on to anything in the past or the uncertain future.

Law of Dependent Origin

Any experience depends on a bunch of preconditions such as our genes, environment, chain of events, actions, perceptions and our mental habits. If an arising condition changes, our experience also will cease to exist in its current form. Nothing stands completely on its own, independent of everything else.

Let us take the example of my beautiful blue kettle. I suffered from the loss because of my craving to have the happy experience of filling it up every morning because of my mental habit of wanting beauty and comfort around me. The kettle does not have an independent identity as a 'beautiful kettle' without certain mental habits (called *sankhara* in Pali) and perceptions (called *sanna* in Pali). Someone else may not find it that charming because their senses may have been conditioned differently. They may notice the glued chipped piece first when they look at my kettle. They may not be so upset if they lose the kettle.

If I become mindful of this chain of dependent conditions, they lose power over me. Although my mental habits will be difficult to change, and my perceptions will need serious re-examination, my mindfulness training now allows me to become aware of and then not let the usual reactions run on autopilot. I can watch the unpleasantness without acting upon my impulses. I can simply watch my own drama and wait for some new conditions to arise such as gratitude for all the enjoyment so far or amusement for my silly little kettle story. I may see my clinging to the kettle in different light—as love for her. This may replace my annoyance to a heart-warming experience. By changing the preconditions mindfully, I am changing the outcome.

Thus, understanding dependent origin through the habit of mindfulness gives us a chance at clinging less to a pre-conceived outcome—and that is non-attachment.

Exercise

Draw whatever comes to your mind and don't label it. Go up to a random set of five people (known or unknown) and ask them to describe what you have drawn in great detail. You are likely to find five different answers because everyone's interpretation is a result of their individual background, mood and outlook. Not one factor can be singled out.

This law has many implications in our daily life:

One way to reduce suffering is to be mindful of the conditions that give rise to it (not just one but all) and work on removing them. Instead of getting angry with someone for hurting us with their words, we may want to become aware of our own prior actions that may have created the hurt. Accept that we typically interpret negative experiences with one-sided view from our perceptions, but there may be more to this story for further exploration. In addition, if we see conditions in their own environment which gave rise to their remarks, it may reduce our judgements of their actions. This may have a cooling effect on the fire of our anger. This is immensely useful in close relationships. Sometimes, even when someone's lifestyle does not affect us directly, we hold judgements against other person's choices in life. Understanding the dependent origin of their way of life is useful for our mental peace and theirs too.

We do not have control over all outcomes because we do not know what chain reactions are happening for the outcome to happen. Sometimes, our experience is like the weather report—hard to predict since it depends on so many different conditions. We can get better at it, but still it is hard to be precise. If so, mindfulness tells us to accept what is happening right now without resisting or getting angry or overreacting. Complete acceptance of the moment is non-attachment to a certain planned outcome. Ironically, such acceptance opens us up to finding new resources to respond to the outcomes.

Karma shows up. Whatever action we are taking today is going to create a ripple effect of desired or undesired results. Wise actions lead to good results. Since we don't always know other preconditions that are taking place, the results may not show up right away or the way we expect them to show up. But we can still execute the part we can control—put in wise actions and wait patiently.

Knowledge of this law breeds humility. It reduces grandiosity of our accomplishments because there is no such thing as a truly 'self-made' person. A series of fortunate events have contributed to it. It allows us to recognise our own privileges and be more inclined to help others who don't have them. Similarly, when something unfortunate happens it may not be fair to attribute the blame to just one thing or person since there are a series of events that lead to the unpleasant event.

We are all connected with each other and affect each other in ways that we may not even know. Hold compassion for each other even when we may not know the people directly. The war in Ukraine is not just a remote war in which we can blame only a certain country or a person. Every time we use Russian gas and oil for our needs, we are contributing to the war.

Implications of the two laws for acknowledging a fluid identity

One very significant implication of the two laws together is that *our identity as a person is not fixed.* Some aspects of it could change (law of impermanence) based on what we are going through and how we process our environment (law of dependent origin). A selfish person can become compassionate if he becomes deeply mindful of the harm he may be doing. A generous person can turn into a bitter one depending on what misfortunes they encounter and how they interpret them. Knowing this could change our attachment to 'me, mine and my ideas' and our interpretation of other people's 'annoying' actions. We may change our intense aversion to that person into acceptance of their personality, background and reactions, leading to fewer conflicts.

When my students first hear about a flexible and shifting identity, they feel restless because statements such as 'This is who I am' or 'This is what I like' no longer ring true. Their identity may be real in that moment, but it is not set in stone. It is subject to change. Be open to that. Being open and accepting the changes that may be coming in is the key to non-attachment.

Internalising this way of thinking will create less attachment to 'me, mine, my ideas' and less hatred of someone for their 'stupid' behaviour because it creates an awareness within us that different journeys can lead to different perceptions. It creates a refuge of 'this too shall pass' when something goes wrong. It inculcates the habit of choosing the right actions today knowing that they will have many implications on many people tomorrow.

Most importantly, when we are not clinging to a desirable outcome, we become open to exploring different ways to tackle it. This opens our perceptions to many possibilities and actions. This leads to creative problem solving and, typically, more constructive solutions.

Meditations and activities for mastering the two laws of non-attachment

We will be outlining two meditations and four activities for deep absorption of the two laws. The first meditation is on mindfulness of body sensations and activities 1 and 2 (tea kettle exercise and savouring the laughter) are for internalising the Law of Impermanence. The second meditation on mindfulness of feelings and thought and activities 3 and 4 (let go of the banana and gain in pain) are meant for internalising the Law of Dependent Origination.

Some of the meditations and activities may be triggering for someone who has had a traumatic experience. If they create anxiety which is too much to handle, stop the meditation for self-care. You can return to it at a later time.

Meditation 1: mindfulness of body sensations

By doing this type of meditation regularly, 'this too shall pass because that is life' becomes a mantra that naturally arises whenever we are experiencing anything difficult. The Pali word for impermanence is *aniccha.* Let aniccha become our mantra. When we go through something that invokes intense emotion in us (negative or positive), we can say to ourselves, 'Aniccha. Aniccha.' At the same time, remember to remember—'I have this moment and I am alive in this moment'.

Meditation 1: Mindfulness of Body Sensations

1. Decide for how long you are going to do this meditation. Set an alarm and attempt to do it for that much time even if you get an urge to stop in the middle.
2. Close your eyes and keep the spinal cord straight.
3. Allow the breath to have its normal pace and notice how the body is receiving the breath. Here and now, in this moment.
4. Notice the whole body, one part at a time, starting at the top of the head and shoulders, back, chest, tummy, upper and lower arms, hands, pelvis, thighs, knees, shins and calves, ankles, feet and toes. Let the attention go to obvious and subtle sensations. Let it flow through the whole body.
5. Notice movement, temperature, tingling, aches, pains and any such direct experience of the sensations.
6. Notice and observe with curiosity how your body sensations are always changing. They are not the same moment by moment. The itching sensation on the skin slowly vanishes if you just let it be and observe it without scratching it. The buzzing sensation in the head may change in intensity. The stomach may have pleasant warm feeling that is different with the in breath and out breath. Accept that 'this is what it is at the moment'. Every time you notice the sensation, you may want to say to yourself, 'aniccha, aniccha'.
7. Do this for as long as you have decided.
8. Take a few deep breaths before letting go of this meditation.

Aha! Moment

Whenever I am enjoying a moment, I can remind myself that this experience is not going to last forever and hence this is the moment to fully experience it. Enjoy the impermanence.

Activity 1: the tea kettle exercise

The case of my missing tea kettle led me to this visualisation exercise.

1. Close your eyes and think about an object (not a person) you really like.

2. Allow yourself to enjoy the object in front of your mind's eye.

3. Notice what type of pleasant feelings are arising.

4. Notice how that enjoyment feels like in the body.

5. Imagine the object disappearing or being destroyed. Choose a not-so-pleasant fate for the object based on your own inclination. In front of your mind's eyes, let this ill fate for the object you love unfold.

6. Pay attention to how your mind reacts to it. What feelings arise? Anxiety? Anger? Sadness? Fear? What thoughts and stories arise? Is there any fear and a temptation to push them away?

Remember, the intention is to come to terms with this in due time.

7. Allow yourself to watch your mind. Keep doing it as long as you are able to.

8. Observe how the intensity and the nature of your feelings and thoughts change.

9. Observe your body sensations to check how *feelings show up in the body*. See if you can hold the discomfort in your body and watch it. Relax your body. Allow yourself to tolerate the discomfort in the body with non-reactivity.

10. Keep saying to yourself, 'This is life or aniccha but I am alive in this moment'. Does any new thought pop up that provides you solace? Do you find yourself feeling a bit desperate? If yes, is it possible to let go of that desperation?

Note: You may not finish this activity in one sitting. But know that you are allowing yourself to come to terms with a loss by getting to know your own mind's power of making up scenarios.

11. Now go back to having the mental image of the object and enjoying it knowing its impermanence. Is the enjoyment different? More or less? Or more peaceful?

12. Stop when you need to. Resume this in your mind whenever you get a chance.

We can do this activity any time we wish when we see an object we really desire, informally. By saying 'aniccha, aniccha' in our mind. Enjoying the object knowing its impermanence, mindfully.

Being non-attached does not mean we don't feel bad when we lose something. It does not mean that we casually or stoically accept the loss. Feelings and thoughts will arise depending on our own patterns but if we are non-attached, we learn to put them in perspective as opposed to spiral down with them. After the initial disappointment, I could watch my mind creating all sorts of scenarios and be amused by them, not feeling despair or fearful or impatient.

Subhashini's story of impermanence

What Swati writes resonates with me. I gained immensely when I applied the Law of Impermanence in my life. Let me share an anecdote.

After two years of living a locked-down life, our little family finally went on a vacation to Greece. Our villa was situated on a coast in Santorini, giving us a first-class view of sunrises and sunsets over the seas and volcanoes. As a family, we laugh a lot, quarrel a lot, and choose to forgive and forget.

As I made scrambled eggs for breakfast and sat on a long wooden table to sip orange juice and relax, I felt nothing but gratitude. Suddenly, my daughter took a bite of her eggs and remarked, 'Mumma! You are the best cook in the world!' The laughter and giggles that followed still vibrate in my ears. At that very moment, I took notice of everything around me—the warm sun, the high tide of the beach and the cold juice. And the sound of our laughter—how relaxed and comfortable we all sounded. I resisted getting up and grabbing my phone to take pictures to post on social media and unnecessarily adding hashtags and filters that may take away from the moment. Simply being aware of our heightened joy and sense of tranquillity made the moment last longer.

It also underlined that nothing is permanent because in a few seconds my daughter had spilt the orange juice and my son was running away with a ball to start playing outside. Nothing is permanent, but you can choose to enjoy it while it lasts.

Thanks, Subhashini. What Subhashini describes can easily be converted into the following activity.

Activity 2: savouring the laughter of impermanence

1. Take a pause when you are enjoying a moment.
2. Pay attention to your feelings in the mind and in the body.
3. Feel grateful for experiencing it.
4. Enjoy the moment as it is unfolding and etch it in your memory.
5. Smile if you feel engulfed with how it is going to end.
6. Smile if you feel something that may *not* be perfect.
7. Savour the moment, and do not obsessively try to capture it with your camera.
8. Notice how you want it to last forever and smile because you know that does not happen.
9. Notice that you have experienced something special and see if it can end there.
10. Smile if your mind is running around to high expectations for the future.
11. Allow yourself to be aware that the same moment will not return. Things are constantly in a state of flux.
12. Return to the *normal* enjoyment of the event if you choose to.

Savouring the joy of impermanence is more than simply smelling the roses here and now. It has the added perspective of not getting stuck on the image of how the enjoyment must look like.

Meditation 2: mindfulness of feelings and thoughts

Follow instructions in the box to the best of your ability.

Meditation 2: Mindfulness of Feelings And Thoughts

1. Close your eyes and keep your spine straight.
2. Allow your breath to have its normal pace and notice how your body is receiving it. Here and now, in this moment.
3. Allow yourself to think about an event that comes to your mind. If it is okay with you to think about a disturbing event, let it come to your mind.
4. If this event is very overwhelming that you are afraid of falling apart, please stop and think about another less disturbing event.
5. Allow the attention to go to the mind. What are you feeling? Anxious, afraid, confused, disappointed? Or something else?
6. Allow yourself to examine your feelings and name the most prominent one.
7. Now pay attention to the thoughts that accompany the feelings. Thoughts are the sentences that come to your mind. For example, say you are feeling angry with a friend who made a disrespectful remark. The feeling is anger. The thoughts could be: *He absolutely disrespects me that he thinks it is okay to hurt me or There is something wrong with me. That's why I get to hear such things from friends.*
8. Now, let go of all the preconceived ideas and thoughts about this matter just for this moment. Allow yourself to have complete openness. As if there is a lot of space in your mind for new thoughts to come up. Just know that if thoughts are unpleasant, instead of pushing them away you want to allow them to be there, knowing that it would help you make sense of the event productively. If it becomes too overwhelming, please allow yourself to stop and revisit some other time.

9. Keep observing the feelings and thoughts and any images that accompany them or the body sensations that arise because of them, as if you are watching a passing train and you are just sitting on the platform watching.
10. There are other possible perspectives to explore. With these possibilities in mind, allow yourself to keep observing the episode being played in your mind. You do not need to actively analyse causes and effects but observing the drama with openness typically gives you epiphanies or a changed perspective.
11. Notice if any new perspective opens up. If it does, the same episode may seem very different.
12. Do this for as long as you need to. To end the meditation, take a few deep breaths and with each breath notice the nourishment that comes in the body.

Remember that this meditation is not meant to actively analyse a situation. You simply observe your feelings and thoughts about a hurtful event. Observing the reality of the situation will offer you insights into the 'dependent origin'. The insights pop into your brain without actively engaging into any frantic analysis. This may not happen in one sitting of the meditation. But having this orientation in mind will allow your brain to work in the background to come up with relevant insights.

Point 10 in the meditation is crucial. For example, you may realise that you had hurt this other person in the past and that may have instigated a remark from him which was equally distressful. Or that the remark really is insignificant when you look at it from that person's perspective. Or that you have a pattern of getting your self-image bruised when a specific type of remark comes to you. Or that you may come to terms with the fact that not everyone is going to like you and that is perfectly okay.

Another realisation may arise in your mind that we are all part of this universe and we are all struggling to make sense of life's events. All these realisations help you not to take the self-image of 'I am hurt' so seriously and instead focus on the fact that each of your action is creating a ripple effect in this world. Hence, you may decide what action to take in the future in a completely different way had it not been for your particular attention to the Law of Dependent Origin.

Observing feelings and thoughts this way frees your mind from getting stuck with a narrow and bothersome perspective. It allows you to come up with new insights into a particular matter. There is nothing independently true in a stand-alone way.

You will find the meditation recordings and guides on www.2meditate.com in the meditations section under 'non-attachment'.

Aha! Moment

In my relationships, opening up my perspective will help me become empathetic and flexible. Otherwise, the tree that does not bend, breaks.

Activity 2: let go of the banana

The famous Indian banana story goes like this: To trap monkeys, the monkey performers set up cages with bars close together with a banana hanging between them. The monkeys in their eagerness to grab the bananas try to get these out of the very close bars so desperately that they do not realise that the hand will not come out as long as it is holding the banana. As a monkey is struggling, the monkey performer goes and grabs the monkey. The monkey is imprisoned because of its intense craving for the banana!

We all have our bananas that entrap us. Typically, they fall into four categories:

1. Body (e.g., body weight, looks, ageing)
2. Finances (e.g., job security, material wants, status and power)
3. Relationships (e.g., partner, friends, relatives, sexual and intimacy desires)
4. Self-image (how the world views us)

Now, carry out this exercise:

1. Think about what your bananas are. Pick one.
2. Close your eyes and imagine that you are a monkey hanging on to that banana. Struggling and maybe even screaming for help.
3. Imagine letting go of that banana. A radical acceptance. Just imagine letting go of the craving. What do you experience? A sense of relief? Anxiety? Fear? Sadness?
4. Just watch it and observe what you are experiencing.
5. This exercise is for simply coming to terms with the lack of complete control we have over making this happen. We don't know all the dependent originations that go into the outcome. We can still survive. We can still be okay and enjoy our life. Know that this radical acceptance may make us use our energy to discover remedies because we are no longer an imprisoned monkey. Take a pause and do this any time intense desire creates misery for you.

Body image: the big banana

Wanting to have a certain type of body with a certain weight has always been a concern for humans, especially women. Lately, this concern seems to have become an obsession. It spans a whole spectrum, from mildly worrying about the body image to being completely miserable about it, ripe with eating disorders. The meteoric rise in procedures and surgeries to make perfect body parts or to overcome the effects of ageing is a big indicator. The standards of an ideal body change but the obsession to get there does not, sometimes even after getting many procedures. The online dating market in which your appearance is what gets you swipes and dates and sustains the dates has made body image into a bigger banana responsible in locking us up in endless misery.

Whether it is Princess Diana—who suffered from eating disorders—or Vidya Balan—who needed to rebel against expectations from fans to be thin—body image has been a big banana for women from all walks of life. Too big to pull out of the cage, set up by the perceived societal expectations, ultimately locking us up in constant misery. Non-attachment to the body image would mean to reduce the misery and obsession. We could have a healthy view of ourselves in spite of desiring a certain body.

Firstly, you must become aware that this is your banana, what it means to let go of it and what do you want to replace the banana with (a healthy alternative that does not imprison you). Say, you are overweight and would like to become thin. Your banana could be 'I absolutely must be thin' and the belief is that 'I cannot be satisfied with my life unless I become thin'. The imprisonment is the constant battle with food or the innumerable tears shed when standing in front of the mirror or the misery felt when a thinner friend gets more attention.

What does it mean to let go of the banana?

Some possibilities include:

- Having a simple desire to lose weight steadily and joyfully.
- Worrying less about approval from people and
- Having appreciation for what works in your life or more confidence in personal and professional environments.

What do you want to replace it with?

Some possibilities include:

- Offering positive affirmation statement like 'people like me because I am funny' each time you feel bad about yourself.
- Practising self-love and self-compassion.
- Wearing clothes and styles that make you feel good about yourself.
- Having a rejoinder ready when you hear any criticism about your weight.

Second, doing the banana exercise often and adding visualisation of what you want to replace it with help. However, quite often, severe body image issues have trauma underneath it. Consider doing trauma work with a specialist to bring down the triggers from the trauma. We can simultaneously do the non-attachment work through the banana exercise. This work takes time but can transform the quality of life.

Aha! Moment

If I know my banana, I can work on letting it go. By contemplating, meditating, 'will-powering', trying it out in real life and trying again and again! Change will show up slowly but surely.

Activity 3: gain from pain

There is nothing comforting about the adage 'No pain, no gain' because it seems like it is glorifying pain. The message feels like—unless you are in pain, you would not learn. Should we invite pain?

Not at all. In fact, the whole idea of non-attachment is not to be stuck in pain. The Law of Dependent Origin suggests that the pain has a cause and an effect.

If we examine the pain, we may get to know its cause and effect and this may give us insights into how to handle it. We may get a completely different perspective and learn about our own strengths to transcend the pain to go towards calmness or even joy.

I will request Subhashini to share her story here.

Thanks, Swati. I was extremely worried about where my life was headed once I quit my flourishing career to be a writer. My friends and family labelling me either 'stupid' or 'brave' for this decision made me want to run away from it. It made me doubt everything and I felt tremendously stuck: I was neither able to write well nor able to happily pursue a career. As I felt stuck, I kept writing as much as I could. Eventually, it made me realise that my passion was my core value and I was fortunate that I was able to honour that. People's approval would follow after my work gets out. Becoming a published author was my gain from this process.

Thanks, Subhashini. When my students participate in this exercise, they experience unexpected things. Try it.

1. Sit in an uncomfortable position.
2. Set the clock and decide that you are going to sit like that for the next five minutes or ten minutes. Set the alarm accordingly.
3. As time goes by, most likely, the discomfort will increase in the beginning.
4. Notice that.
5. Notice what your mind starts to tell you.
6. See if you can still be open to observing the stories and perspectives that your mind is telling you.
7. See what you learn about the reaction to the pain.
8. Stick around until you hear the alarm.
9. Notice what came to you. Did any insightful thought come to you? Did you gain anything from the pain? Or this time around was it just pain and nothing more?

Any time you are going through a difficult emotion or pain, you may want to think about this exercise. If you choose to let the emotion run its course, you may come to terms with it and notice the gain.

Last time I did this exercise and watched my physical discomfort, I suddenly remembered the time when I had developed an unusual eye infection. I felt embarrassed not only because it looked bad, but also because I felt I did not have a robust immune system. I recalled how for my family of origin it was a point of pride to be healthy and robust. I was uneasy because my body had not avoided an infection.

I realised that the pain had disturbed my self-image that I should have no health issues because somehow, I had inherited great genes and also, I had a healthy lifestyle. After this realisation, I made a conscious choice to not judge myself nor anyone for their physical ailments. How silly, I thought, to hold people responsible for every physical problem they experienced. Had they any control over their physical condition, they would exert that control and would have a better time.

There are limitations people have over removing conditions, including things like being overweight or impulsivity. I felt compassion for all sorts of conditions. It felt right not to hold judgements against me and others for whatever difficulties we may be experiencing. A big insight.

These are the ways in which we can actively cultivate non-attachment. Coming to terms with pain in life—not running away from difficulties and not clinging to pleasant experiences but simply enjoying them. This way, we do not need to stop ourselves from fully engaging in life because we know we can manage beautifully the inevitable difficulties by acquiring the power of non-attachment.

7
How Non-Attachment Fuels Passion

A Deep Dive into Dharma

'I want to sing like the birds sing, not worrying about who hears or what they think.'

—Rumi

Zen and the art of chasing ambition

Shelley and Monica were best friends. Both were excellent students and had a thriving social life in Mumbai. At the age of seventeen, Shelley moved to the US for higher studies and Monica stayed back to join her family business.

Shelley's father was an ardent vipassana practitioner who had influenced her in attending two 10-day vipassana retreats before heading for the US and adopting mindfulness early in her life and career path.

Monica, on the other hand, believed it was all mumbo-jumbo and nothing could compromise hard work and fiery attitude to achieving her career goals.

Watching Monica aggressively invest in her family business, Shelley started feeling conflicted about her father's advice about staying on the path of mindfulness regardless of what career path she chose. The question she was struggling to answer was: *If I am too zen, will I lose my ambition and passion*?

By 'too zen', she meant too laid-back to chase her career goals.

Four years passed. Shelley graduated from college with a degree in psychology (much to her parents' chagrin who wanted her to study business). Not only did she pass with flying colours but she also had made friends for life.

Despite the restrictions on immigrants for getting non-science/tech jobs, Shelley managed to find a job in her chosen field. All seemed rosy and Shelley seemed to have achieved what she wanted to do.

> ***'A burning passion coupled with absolute non-attachment is the key to all success.'***
> **Mahatma Gandhi**

Across the world in Mumbai, Monica had set up additional retail stores for her family business to showcase the new garments and designs they had produced. Both girls were very successful until Covid-19 struck. Shelley lost her job. Her father wanted her to return and help him in their family business. That seemed like the easy way out as she could be living a comfortable life back home in Mumbai. She struggled to decide because she knew managing the family business is not what she wanted to do.

On the other hand, Monica's business was struggling to stay afloat in the Covid times. She had to close half of the new stores and had to dissolve personal assets to pay off loans. Both had stayed true to their passion but were now facing challenges for staying on the path.

Shelley went into a three-day self-enforced mindfulness retreat in her own studio apartment. She did all her mindfulness activities and meditation, cooked her own food and stayed silent. After three days, she had made up her mind to stay in the US and find a job to pay for her dream of doing a PhD in psychology.

She risked her relationship with her father but stayed focused and continued in her job search. Even with dwindling savings, she kept telling herself, 'This too shall pass'. She accepted the occasional feelings of being low and depressed as part of the path and did not desperately fight to get out of them at any cost.

She persevered for a job with determination to endure. In a couple of months, she was able to get another job and even started another part-time position to accumulate funds for her PhD. She knew that her focus, resilience and insight into what she should do came from her mindfulness practice. She could finally answer her own question: *My zen is indeed the biggest support for staying with my passion*!

Monica on the other hand, had been aggressive with her investments in the business and now was aggressively chasing illegal lenders to keep the business afloat. Her passion and ambition to keep the business alive was blinding her to wrong decisions and having completely taken over, she did not heed to her parents' and relatives' advice either.

A year into the pandemic, Monica realised her mistakes and eventually decided to marry another businessman who, although a stranger, agreed to buy out her business in exchange for her hand.

Two best friends. Two different passions and two different paths. Both hit rock bottom. But one survived the hard path and the other chose a less fulfilling life.

How to be strategic while pursuing passion

In popular culture, mindfulness is supposed to give us a 'zen-like' quality. A halo that keeps us almost always calm, composed, controlled and not perturbed by any chaos or emotional storm that goes on around us.

My friends often tell me, 'You are the mindfulness coach. You are not supposed to get stressed out. You are almost always content, 'being nice' to everybody, hardly ever getting angry and almost never doing anything unwise.'

A mindful person is supposed to be perpetually thoughtful, not impulsive and is not supposed to get carried away with emotions.

On the contrary, a red-hot passionate person is painted as someone consumed by single-minded pursuit of their passion who neither cares about their surroundings, nor is aware of anything other than what they are chasing. Their passion may drive them to impulsive actions.

They may forget eating, sleeping or treating people right. The mad scientist with a beautiful mind or a genius artist in a gale and yet painting or an entrepreneur who is willing to bribe and even go to jail because they so madly want to get the contract.

There is a big problem with both cases described above—they are extreme. The mindful zen person sounds like a completely enlightened being, a notion that is simply aspirational (like the Zen Master Hakuin*)*. Pema Chodron asserts mindful householders will retain the crazy mess they find themselves in with more regulated emotions, patience, focus and awareness.

A red-hot person most likely would not want to be a Van Gogh in their temperament. They would benefit from mindfully managing their emotions and still retaining their passion.

What most do not realise is that there are people who are passionate and mindful. They are *strategic*, pursuing passion with focus and mindful awareness.

How to engage with our passions without attachment

'If I practise mindfulness, will I lose my ambition? Will I not have that burning passion?'

I often get to hear this question from my students.

Mindfulness practice does *not* dilute our passion, but it changes the means we use to pursue it. We learn to follow the passion with complete engagement and not with harmful attachment.

The question arises because of the way we may misunderstand and use the word attachment. Having a strong desire to achieve a goal is not attachment! If we *cling* to the desire in a destructive way, it is attachment. Non-attachment allows complete engagement without clinging. Engagement has the quality of checks and balances that we are not spreading deliberate harm in the world. *Attachment does not.*

Engagement holds an awareness of one's actions. Attachment is an autopilot reaction for self-preservation. Do the hard work of getting to the goal without clinging to the final reward.

Here is an example of how to follow your passion with engagement and non-attachment:

An entrepreneur is consumed by wanting to be successful. She virtually sleeps in the office and has no social life. She puts in a lot of hard work without that much pay-off, and feels burned out and cannot take the deprived life any longer. If she jumps off to 'plan B', not because of some vital strategic reason but because she is exhausted, it is attachment. If she is able to practise a 'steady do it' attitude in spite of the ups and downs and keeps working on her start-up possibly with new learnings, it is engagement.

1. If you are experiencing unhealthy anxiety that is compromising your own and your family's health while pursuing the job of your dreams or a passion, you may want to ask yourself: What am I addicted to? If the answer is 'glorifying my self-image', it is attachment. If the answer is 'I want to do a good job of what I have taken up', you may be able to change your perspective and enjoy the moment of working towards that goal. That is engagement.

2. If you are willing to harm others to realise your dreams, it is attachment. If you have convictions about your good work and are following that path in spite of judgements from others, it is engagement. Some Buddhist monks resorted to violence and connived to promote their own version of Buddha's teachings. This is attachment, not engagement. In fact, Buddha himself always told his disciples to believe his teachings only after practising and realising their benefits. Ill will towards others creates harm perpetuated by more harm in the long run.

How to practise engagement through mindfulness

Consider this.

You may be sitting on the meditation cushion watching your body sensations for hours despite discomfort and a strong wish to get up and go. Your wandering attention will need to be brought back. You are training to focus. You are also learning about your bodily sensations and you are learning not to panic.

What you learn: Focusing with self-discipline.

You may be drinking a few sips of tea mindfully despite the morning rush or the anxiety of starting another day. You are changing your autopilot reaction towards feeling less anxious. You are learning to appreciate the tea even when it may not be as hot as you want. When it is a perfect cup of tea, you are full of joy and gratitude.

What you learn: Enjoying the pleasant and the unpleasant without reacting.

When your phone makes a WhatsApp beep, you may be fighting your instinct to pick up the phone and may be making sure to take one mindful deep breath before extending your arm.

What you learn: Changing your lifelong habits of yielding to impulsive habits.

You may wash dishes by paying attention to every touch of the soapsuds and notice how this mundane activity can be pleasurable. A wandering mind is an unhappy mind.

What you learn: How a meaningful moment can be felt even with a mundane activity.

You may be placing your hand on the heart area when you are going through a difficult feeling, acknowledging that it is hard to go through and let yourself feel it for some time. When you feel stress, you may sit quietly and watch your body with curiosity saying, 'Oh! Stress feels like this in this body at this moment'. You are not quickly pushing difficult feelings away.

What you learn: Watching the reality may bring new knowledge on how to react effectively as opposed to reacting impulsively.

You may be doing meditation to be aware of feelings with open awareness. Watch what comes in your sphere of attention. In doing so, you are learning the art of getting a different perspective on things. Not having rigid ideas on how to solve an issue but to be open and to increase your span of world view.

What you learn: New ideas, new solutions, new interpretations, new questions may fill up your mind. You learn to unlearn and experience the freedom to think and feel!

You may be thinking about the banana you cling to while doing the letting go exercise and realise either with a calm mind or a heavy heart that you have been investing too long in a toxic relationship or a loss-making business or nearly impossible goals.

What you learn: When to let go. When to give up on a particular road to the pursuit of passion and still accept the aftermath of the decision. Possibly allowing new roads to be explored.

What mindfulness does to your brain

'Mindfulness practice can literally change your brain.'

Sara Lazar, neuroscientist

Research conducted by two neuroscientists for the *Harvard Business Review* shows that doing mindfulness meditations impacts brain structure. In practitioners, it instigates increased activity in the anterior cingulate cortex (ACC), a part of the brain that regulates emotions and mood. This region is associated with self-regulation and learning from past experiences.

Compared to non-meditators, mindfulness meditators (typically after eight weeks of training) show superior performance in resisting distractions, making optimal decisions and regulating emotional ups and downs. Neuroscientists have also shown that practising mindfulness affects brain areas related to perception, body awareness, pain tolerance, emotion regulation, introspection, complex thinking and sense of the self.

'Mindfulness should no longer be considered a "nice-to-have" for executives. It's a "must-have", a way to keep our brains healthy, to support self-regulation and effective decision-making capabilities and to protect ourselves from toxic stress.'

—Christina Congleton, Britta Holzel, Sara Lazar, *Harvard Business Review*, 8 January 2015

How pursuing your passion is your dharma

Aryan, one of my mindfulness students, went through the angst of choosing between a well-paying prestigious corporate job with a good trajectory and following his passion for being a musician.

As is true with most high-achieving individuals, he had anxiously put more than 100 per cent of himself in everything he took up and always strived for perfection. After starting mindfulness practice, the angst was different because he chose to stay with the confusion instead of following the safe path of keeping the corporate job.

As he was struggling with it for many weeks, he realised that up until then he had avoided pain by creating a distance between himself and the issue by quickly reassuring himself that 'everything is going to be just great' and desperately looking at the silver lining too fast.

As a perpetual optimist, he had always tried to mask the pain of achieving a new goal with his positivity. But now he realised that by doing that, he was stopping himself from taking the risk of following his passion.

He became aware of his attachment to external validations that came to him in the form of 'awards, achievements and consumerism'. Aryan was attached to wanting to be perfect in everything. He was attached to his self-image and self-glory as opposed to simply pursuing the passion—his dharma—which would bring him meaning.

Switching to his passion of becoming a musician and taking the risk with awareness would be complete engagement, not attachment or red-hot passion. But to expect perfection in every activity to prove himself to the world would be attachment. That creates humongous pressure and anxiety without offering a real meaning.

When it starts raining, you can choose to lock yourself in a safe place and watch the rain. This is really detachment. What if you choose to stay in the rain and open your umbrella and still allow yourself to experience the rain? Sometimes it would be simply beautiful and sometimes you may get your elbows wet. You are creating a distance but you are still part of the rain.

The umbrella is non-attachment. Complete engagement is enjoying whatever life brings us (including the muddy part), while keeping ourself dry.

Is self-glory so bad?

Let us face it. Following our passion may not always be only because we believe in doing a good job (following our dharma). We have selfish motivations like interest in proving our worth to the rest of the world, promoting self-interests or wanting to be better than others.

On the whole spectrum of self-glory, one toxic end of the spectrum may be completely selfish and power-hungry behaviour and the other end of the spectrum may be wanting to be valued and respected.

On the one hand, hunger for self-glory creates dictators, exploitative gurus and abusive CEOs and on the other hand, the need for recognition and respect is almost universal. It can motivate us to achieve and to make a difference. So, it is not always bad. However, attachment to 'how I must look to the world around me' can create suffering. How does one balance that?

To answer this, we can look at the developmental stages of human life for perspective.

Everything has a right time, attachment to self-glory and non-attachment to it. Non-attachment to self-glory is more appropriate if cultivated as we go through life's developmental phases. It may fail if prematurely imposed. This view of development is supported by Western psychology as well as ancient Indian philosophy of life, in slightly different ways.

Understanding self-glory through the prism of Indian philosophy

In Indian philosophy, a lifespan is divided into four consecutive parts called ashram. Each phase is characterised by what the person is expected to do.

In the first part, a person is advised to be a student and acquire appropriate skills. This part of life is called *Brahmacharyashram* translated as 'celibate student'. Possibly a more self-driven stage.

In the second part of life, a person is supposed to raise a family by immersing in making a living and collecting resources. In this phase, the individual is supposed to be more invested in caring for their family. This phase is called *Garhasthyashram* translated as 'householder'.

In the third phase of life, a person begins to retire and help their offspring to raise their children and get settled in their lives. This is the time to pull back from collecting resources and get ready for a spiritual life. This phase is called *Vanaprasthashram* translated as 'returning to the forest'.

In the last part of life, a person is advised to move away from the worldly pleasures and move towards spiritual life. The path to do this is by renunciation of material goods and begin the process of transcending into understanding other-worldliness. This phase is called *Sanyasashram* translated as 'renunciation'.

These phases are neither to be taken as 'prescriptions', nor to be followed in the same order. However, one can take it as a recognition that in each developmental stage, our focus may shift and non-attachment can provide tremendous help in this shift in the right direction.

During Brahmacharyashram, a young student's motivation to acquire skills may come more for *self-glory* or for proving oneself to the world and that is perfectly okay as a foundation.

Cultivating non-attachment is useful during Garhasthyashram as one begins to care for the family because then the motivation to achieve would shift from 'self' to doing the work well. Unless we understand non-attachment to self-glory, this is the phase most likely to create harmful power-hungry behaviour.

In the third phase, the non-attachment would continue to shift the focus away from 'me, mine and my ideas', to handing over the reins to the next generation. Unless the focus shifts away from 'me', a lot of conflict can arise as seen in the form of two generations feuding with each other to grab power.

This is the time when we benefit from ageing gracefully. Sanyasashram is the time when it is tremendously helpful to accept that our place in the world is becoming less relevant. Although we may want to preserve our health and vitality as much as possible, clinging to the past glory in desperation creates unhappy old people.

Non-attachment in the last phase, as a result, would include letting go of material pleasures and shifting to contemplation and wisdom. This aspect of the Indian phase of life is most rejected by the modern times in which 'youth preservation' has become the preferred choice. Non-attachment in the last phase of life includes accepting death and preparing for a graceful exit.

In Western psychology, although the renunciation of the material pleasures as we mature is not advised explicitly, the mature life is supposed to be moving towards community interests as opposed to self-interests.

Viewing self-glory through the prism of two popular Western theories

Two most popular and commonly cited theories from Western psychology on human development through the lifespan are from Maslow and Erikson. Abraham Maslow's extended '8-stage hierarchy of needs' was first presented in his 1954 book *Motivation and Personality* and later revised. Erik

Erikson's 'eight stages of psycho-social human development' first published in 1950 is still relevant and most influential on how human life evolves by experiencing conflicts at different stages in life.

In Maslow's hierarchy of needs, after the self-oriented needs are met, a person seeks personal growth and going beyond personal self into fulfilment and possibly spiritual experiences. In Erikson's model, in the last two phases of development, if things go well, a human being becomes less preoccupied with personal gain and more interested in family and community. It involves acceptance of life in its fullness, including the good and the bad. This sounds like engagement in life without clinging to a certain expectation. The result is wisdom.

Although non-attachment is not explicitly prescribed to reach wisdom in these theories, life is supposed to move from 'me' to a bigger circle that includes spirituality. Although it is sensible to honour the developmental need for personal resource collection early in life as described in these theories, the drive towards wisdom of non-attachment is also implicitly included as a person grows older. In the scheme of life proposed in this book, I would urge the reader to become familiar with non-attachment early in life and then allow it to flourish in practice as we mature. Not to wait for the age to show its wisdom to appear. It will offer the raft for floating in turbulent waters, no matter what phase of life we are in. Our passion may come from the need for 'self-glory' in the early part of life but we can still use the raft of non-attachment when needed. As we mature, we can allow it to be transferred to the need for following our dharma, we will be able to collect the wisdom Erikson proposed or the self-actualization Maslow suggested.

Shelley's dilemma resolved

Let us revisit Shelley's story. We may recall that Shelly had a wish to pursue PhD in psychology. Eventually, she expressed this desire to her vipassana teacher who asked her about her motivation behind it. Was it based on a wish for personal glory? He advised her to go beyond her ego and look for a profession that helps others. This confused her.

My advice for Shelley would be slightly different. She must follow her desire to do her PhD even if it is for personal glory, since she is still a young person driven by the wish to establish herself. The subject of her PhD is something her heart yearned for, this may be her dharma. Since she is already introduced to the idea of non-attachment, she is more likely to move into the direction of non-attachment to 'self-glory'.

Non-attachment—the key to pursuing passion

'Don't just live a life; build one.' **—Steve Jobs**

We can follow our passion at any age and stage of life. We can be like Harbhajan Kaur who started selling signature home-made *besan ki barfi* at the age of ninety. We can leave a legacy without starting a family like Lata Mangeshkar. Life is too short to sacrifice any dream, just make it happen and feel the change.

If we cultivate the practice of non-attachment, we will be able to sustain that passion with focus and engagement. A youngster's motivation and ambition to do well could be an attachment to how they look at the world. It may move towards possessing luxurious assets, moving from owning a Kinetic to a BMW.

But if we cultivate non-attachment at that time, just imagine how it will help us engage with our passion, sustain relationships, manage stress, anxiety and ambition differently. Let your imagination run wild here.

Non-attachment—the core of passionate leadership

When talking about passion and success in the same sentence, the first name that comes to mind is Steve Jobs. His passion for marrying technology and art reflected in the products he created from the first MacBook to the iPod and the iPhone. Nothing short of revolutionary and path-breaking.

As Walter Isaacson writes, it was Steve Jobs's intensity that tied his personality with the products he invented. 'This intensity encouraged a binary view of the world. Something was either "best thing ever" or it was shitty, brain-dead,' writes Isaacson in his book *The Exclusive Biography*. Interestingly, Jobs attributed his love for simplicity in his product designs to his zen training.

However, this zen training never produced in him a zen-like calm or inner serenity. 'He made a point of being brutally honest which made him charismatic and inspiring, yet also, to use the technical term, an asshole at times.' Could it be that Jobs was attached to the work done exactly the way he imagined but not attached to self-glory or people pleasing?

When Jobs was thrown out from Apple, he locked himself in his house for three days. His zen practice—which is a form of mindfulness practice—gave him the clarity he needed for the next step. He went on to reinventing the music and animation industry.

Contrary to Jobs' leadership style is another successful executive who has made mindfulness, meditation and non-attachment a part of his business ethos—Marc Benioff, Salesforce Co-CEO.

Salesforce offices have a mindfulness zone on each floor, where employees set their phones aside and take a quiet moment. Since innovation is at the core of Salesforce, Benioff focuses on creating a 'beginner's mind'. The beginner's mind is a Buddhist philosophy that encourages curiosity, openness and lack of judgement.

Mindfulness in the company's culture has helped lower employee burnout that is accompanied by a sense of attachment to results but still cultivates the passion to continuously innovate.

One of Benioff's most important principles is that in business, trust is more important than growth. 'If you put growth above trust, all of a sudden you create a toxic culture,' Benioff said. 'People don't want to work in that environment or use the product.'

Two contrasting styles of successful leadership with passion—one practised mindfulness for clarity in decision-making and the other one for putting people and trust ahead of growth.

Non-attachment—the foundation of passionate relationship

Most of us want a 'happily ever after' with our partner of choice and likely label that as a successful relationship because of its longevity and its contribution to happiness.

Attached (clingy) love motivates you to measure the success of your relationship in earthly measurements: Did my boyfriend buy me gifts for Valentine's Day? Has my husband made my friends his? Does my girlfriend know how to prioritise work and time with me? Unfortunately, love attached to outcomes and expectations hardly last.

Non-attachment is at the core of forming relationships that last beyond the initial infatuation. It makes us accept that love in the relationship can fluctuate, be threatened and yet, relished whole-heartedly. It increases the chances that we will be able to accept our partner and fight the odds to be together.

So, whether it is our passion for a task, skill, creative endeavour, science discovery, connections with people, a special relationship or anything else, non-attachment does not take it away but changes the way we pursue it with a 'steady does it' attitude.

Aha! Moment

Non-attachment turns me into a tortoise in the race to my ambition. The hare may get a head start but the tortoise finishes the race.

SECTION 4

Core Values

8

How Core Values Satisfy the Human Search for Meaning

In Pursuit of Well-Being, Not Happiness

'The secrets of Dharma are hidden in the heart's cave.'
—Mahabharata, 3:117:313

Let your core values be the guiding light

Rewind to 2005. I felt so stretched in all directions. I wanted it all—a flourishing career, a happy family with two kids and an intimate relationship with my husband. Raising a young nuclear family in the US without any family help can be demanding.

To maintain an intimate relationship with my husband, time and mental energy was needed. To top it all, this was my second career and that put an additional pressure to establish myself firmly in my newly chosen field. At the same time, I had a lot of other interests such as films, arts, fitness and shopping—and I was going bonkers trying to fit it all in my busy schedule.

I was used to getting validations and attention from friends and family but being so stretched, I felt completely devoid of that attention. I felt I was not doing anything that well any more. This bred stress and irritability, pushing people further away.

The 'me first' attitude that had given me an exciting life when I was single and successful was becoming a liability now.

This was the time when I had just begun my mindfulness journey. I had to spend time on my practice to get a sense of resolution. Sitting in meditations, with time carved out with enough preparation to make it happen, I struggled to identify what I valued the most.

Years of habits needed to be broken to mindfully observe what the reality was. After a lot of attempts at observing the physical and mental pain, my feelings and thoughts started changing. My core value finally dawned on me—it was being my family's anchor.

I felt responsible for two young lives and their growth in this world. My husband was good at getting things done when I specifically asked him but outside of that his real energy was spent in the academic world of ideas and research.

Once I zeroed on my core value it felt right in my heart, and I did not care if it was because of my upbringing or if it was against my feminist beliefs. I had to honour my core value. And the best part? It did not feel like a compromise or an adjustment.

After that, the importance of all other things fell into place. I continued to work but scaled back expectations for a few years and that felt alright. The need for external validations through career and the desire to look good and successful did not seem as important.

And when that need died down, it seemed alright to let go of it. Some in my social circle disapproved of my choice and some applauded it. Others' opinions ceased to matter.

My story is not at all to tell women to choose family over career when kids are young. My story is to say that when we are faced with difficult choices, it helps to make our core values our guiding light.

What are core values?

> ***'Open your arms to change, but don't let go of your values.'***
>
> **—Dalai Lama**

Core values are values that feel right to us beyond the wants of that moment. They are based on what we think is important to us and add a sense of purpose to our actions. Core values respond to our quest for meaning. We have the innate need to find meaning in life. Pleasure gained by every passing moment is fleeting. The present-moment awareness brings us the joy of the moment and teaches us how to relieve stress.

However, that alone is not enough for planning the necessities of our modern life with work, family, passion, financial security and relevance in the world we live in. We are constantly required to make decisions—small and big. Core values help us make the *right* decisions that honour our need for meaning and purpose. It is our guiding light.

If we ignore our core values, our decisions are made out of habit, as a result not always wise. For a lot of things in life, this works in the short run. Even avoiding an issue works for some time. But at some point in life, we are faced with that issue head-on and need to make a constructive choice. At that point, we can rely on our core values.

A seven-point deep dive into core values

As we practise present moment awareness with non-attachment, we objectively learn about our habits and patterns to know what gives us the most solace. This understanding of our reality, coupled with the intention of letting go of greed and aversion, puts us in touch with the part of us that may be starving for nourishment and also the part of us that is capable of providing nourishment. As we begin to see what gives us wholesome nourishment that alleviates the distress, core values begin to emerge.

Examples of Core Values

- *Financial independence*
- *Helping others*
- *Compassion*
- *Kindness*
- *Emotional independence*
- *Self-discovery*
- *Honesty*
- *Integrity*
- *Family*
- *Spiritual journey*
- *Harmony*
- *Gratitude*

Core values are not goals

Goals and core values are different. Goals are things we want to achieve. Core values can guide us into making choices while pursuing our goals.

A businessperson may choose not to bribe a government official to get a contract because their core value is integrity. The contract may be difficult to clinch because of the core value but adherence to it will allow the person to sleep peacefully.

On the other hand, if providing for the family is a core value for someone, they may choose to bribe the government official for securing the contract without which the financial difficulties would mount. They may still sleep peacefully knowing that they are fulfilling their core value.

However, if a businessperson wants to become successful *at any cost* as this is his core value and in the process creates harm (for example, Ponzi scheme), it is not core value but greed.

Core values are difficult to live by

Living according to our core values may not make us happy all the time but it gives us a sense of purpose that makes the difficulties worthwhile. If we pursue the sensation of *feeling good* alone, we get bored and lose meaning. The hedonic treadmill makes us exhausted and dissatisfied.

What offers us salvage is *well-being*. This version of happiness is what most happiness researchers/experts talk about, including Martin Seligman (author of *Flourish*), Raj Raghunathan (happiness researcher), His Holiness the Dalai Lama and Buddha.

Illiterate Savitri got married to Jyotiba Phule when she was 10 years old in 1840. Jyotiba taught her reading and writing and then encouraged her to get teacher's training from a missionary organisation. He believed in equal rights to education for women and Dalits, at a time when this was condemned because it was supposed to be against the teachings in *Manusmriti*.

Jyotiba's parents threw the couple out of their house because they had established girls' schools. They both moved to a friend's house where Savitri met her future friend and colleague, Fatima Sheikh. Together they established educational trusts for educating Dalits. Both Jyotiba and Savitribai Phule lived by their core values with immense difficulty. Their names are written in the annals of history for their contribution to girls' education in India and for combating untouchability and uplifting the lower castes through education and awareness campaigns.

Core values can change

Core values are not cast in stone. With age and changing circumstances, new values can emerge and sometimes replace the old ones.

In 2010, David Blankenhorn was asked to be an expert witness in *Perry vs Schwarzenegger* in California to oppose legalising gay marriages. Schwarzenegger was the governor of the state of California then. Blankenhorn is a respected author, activist and founder of National Fatherhood Initiative promoting responsible fatherhood.

He vehemently opposed gay marriages on the grounds that 'children had a right to be cared for by the two biological parents'. His value was to uphold the institution of marriage for children's right. However, in 2012 he wrote an opinion piece in the *New York Times* stating that his stance on legalising gay marriage has changed.

He realised that his value of equal rights to all was paramount and that included dignity to homosexual love. This would require legalising gay marriage to make it truly equal. David had observed that with time, the attitudes of Americans had changed towards gay relationships and many youngsters favoured gay marriages. He respected this change that came along with time.

Core values may not fit the social norms

What we value may not look good to others or may not fit the norms of society. However, we live by it because they feel *right* to us.

Buddha honoured his core value of *searching for answers to human suffering* when he was a young prince called Siddhartha.

To his father's great disappointment, instead of choosing to inherit the kingdom, he gave up his own family and royal life. His act did not fit the social norms by any means; however, Siddhartha was honouring his core value. This act was not done with the intention to harm his family but to seek the well-being of the entire mankind.

Core values are not intentionally harmful to others or to us

> ***'Do not use the wrong means to do good work.'***
> **—Jyotiba Phule**

What if a serial killer says that his innate desire is to kill people? Can we say that by honouring his desire he is upholding his core value? In the world of mindfulness, we seek well-being by observing the moment with non-attachment and compassion. Compassion increases our awareness of our own and others' pain. Innately, we all have the ability to spread goodness.

We need to make sure that we are not intentionally harming others or causing distress while pursuing our core values.

Seventeen-year-old Gauri Maulekhi almost fainted at the sight of a maggot-infested dog in a veterinarian camp in Lucknow. Since that time, she was so motivated to protect animals from neglect and cruelty, she became an animal activist and worked on several projects such as creating the first animal shelter in the city.

She lobbied in Nepal to end the mass animal slaughter in Gadhimai festival. Although she won the Nari Shakti Puraskar award in 2018, her activism was not approved by many as people tend to be afraid of getting bitten by stray dogs. Most people believe that the country's limited resources need to be used for humans first.

These concerns are valid too; however, what makes the animal rights campaign successful is the heart-felt intention to address cruelty. If such work is done with animosity and violence, it creates acrimony and misunderstandings, not compassion.

Abortion rights activists who harm doctors or animal rights activists who torment scientists who use animals for their experiments are people with misguided core values.

But if core value is practised without any harmless intention, the activist will be able to work on the cause without resorting to violence.

Core values can conflict with each other

If being honest and not hurting another person are your core values, they may conflict with each other when the honest feedback will hurt the other person's feelings. If honouring professional skills and caring for family are your core values and when there is a conflict between the two it may give rise to guilt or shame unless you mindfully contemplate on the resolution by sometimes accepting your own limitations.

Core values are not obvious and need to be discovered

Core values are not always obvious unless one struggles to realise them. Self-awareness with non-attachment helps to identify core values. The following chapter has exercises to discover our core values.

East or West, core values test

Core values satisfy human search for meaning and this is discussed in the East and the West in the following three ways:

1. Buddha's teachings,
2. Dharma as defined in the Bhagavad Gita and
3. Research on happiness in the West.

The core of Buddha's Noble Eightfold Path

Without the discussion of core values from Buddha's teachings, mindfulness could become a mechanical and mundane tool for momentary stress reduction.

In order to cultivate non-attachment to greed and hatred and for reducing suffering for us and others, Buddha suggested an eightfold path, which is the foundation of Buddhist ethics. In Buddhism, ethics are understood by the term *sila* in Pali. Out of the eightfold factors, three are called sila factors, directly aligned with core values:

1. Wise speech,
2. Wise actions and
3. Wise livelihood.

The sila factors were taught by Buddha not as morality lessons (wrongs and rights), but as a way to purify our mind and move towards a sense of well-being. They reduce our anxiety and fear because they give us meaning and courage even when things are difficult. Following sila gives us courage. This is an essential step on a spiritual path to end our suffering.

Essentials of wise speech

'If only our tongues were made of glass, how much more careful we would be when we speak.'—Shaun Shane

Wise (or skilful) speech is my favourite sila factor because it has immensely helped me in my relationships.

Wise speech is

1. not lying,
2. not gossiping,
3. not disliked by others and
4. not harmful to others.

This by itself sounds obvious because this advice is doled out by parents during our childhood and has become part of our non-conscious value system. It may even sound clichéd, but when we pay conscious attention to it, we feel uncomfortable about not practising it. We realise that it is complicated to practise, in fact almost impossible, just like the examples below. They show us why we need to carefully think about the reasons for our unwise speech and think about when and why to change it into wise speech.

Wise speech includes not lying.

'So sorry I cannot come to your event tomorrow because I need to go to my aunt's place for a family thing that I cannot avoid. I am so bummed!'

The real reason is that you don't like this friend and really don't want to go to that event and plan to stay at home and watch Netflix instead.

'I am not cheating on you! I am just being friends. I am a friendly person. He is not special to me any more.'

A wife telling her husband about meeting her ex because she fears the truth coming out.

'The company is doing excellent as shown by the profits going up this quarter.'

The CEO of a company instead of admitting to the accounting gimmicks may lie to keep the stock prices up.

Truth eventually catches up and we find our friend confronting us for the excuses, a husband catching his cheating wife red-handed and business scams exposed by whistle-blowers.

To keep the facade that everything is fine is so ingrained in us that lying about the reality seems like part of the game of life.

With pressures to look fortunate in front of others, we are trained to show that things are normal. And when something happens out of the ordinary, we gossip about that person or incident.

Wise speech includes not gossiping or backbiting.

> ***'Great minds discuss ideas, average minds discuss events, small minds discuss people.'***
>
> **—Eleanor Roosevelt**

We know how much we enjoy the reality shows on TV full of gossip, cat fights and drama. The phenomenal success of *Keeping Up With the Kardashians* and *Fabulous Lives of Bollywood Wives* is proof of how we engage in celebrity gossip without even knowing them.

How much we judge others shows how we need to feel superior to others or compensate for our feeling inferior. Unfortunately, being non-judgemental is not natural to humans.

Wise speech includes not disliked by others.

There are many instances when we say things disliked by others, intentionally or inadvertently. As an employer, we need to communicate incompetence clearly or even fire a person. Fights between people who are intimate with each other are supposed to be an essential part of intimacy, but fights make us say things that are unpleasant ad even hurtful to the other.

But there are times when saying unpleasant facts are essential for the good of the person. A teacher's feedback, even when irksome, could be life altering in a good way. Coaching kids when they need to learn life's skills can be bothersome and difficult but essential for the child's social fitness.

Wise speech includes not harming others.

Unfortunately, when we experience anger and frustration we intentionally harm with our words. Unless we are trained, we express it to the person who has hurt us with the intention of 'giving it back to them'. We have feelings of revenge which we express in harmful speech and other actions. If we have undergone bitter experiences or trauma ourselves, we are triggered and say things that can have long-term harmful effects on others.

As children, our parents may take it out on us through hurtful words and we may hold on to that forever shamefully. Not ill-treating others is a practice that we need to truly believe in and keep cultivating by making a note of when we end up violating that value.

How do we respond to the difficulties in wise speech?

There are two factors that form the foundation to practising wise speech—right time and compassion. Wise speech does not mean *never say things disliked by others.* If we have compassion in our heart for the other person and if we are saying it at the right time, it is wise speech.

If we know that our blunt speech would benefit the other, we would say them at the right time and in the right way. If we have compassion in our heart, we would not want to hurt others intentionally by taking revenge or taking our own bitterness out on others.

In 2019, a shooting killed fifty people in two mosques in the city of Christchurch. Leaders in Germany and France responded to the attacks by saying they will not be intimidated and will get back with equal rage. But Prime Minister of New Zealand Jacinda Ardern covered her head, met with the grieving families and said, 'Many of those who will have been directly affected by this shooting may be migrants to New Zealand;

they may even be refugees here. They have chosen to make New Zealand their home and it is their home. They are us. The person who perpetuated violence is not. They have no place in New Zealand (the *Guardian,* 15 March 2019).'

In less than a week after the attack, she spoke to her Parliament and announced a ban on military-sized weapons. Ardern revolutionised the way Western leaders respond to terror and the words they use in their public speeches. She sought the right words at the right time and delivered it with compassion. And followed it up with the right actions.

Essentials of wise action

Buddha said that our core values must be reflected in our actions. Wise actions include:

1. no killing intentionally,
2. no stealing or taking away what is not yours and
3. no sexual misconduct.

Of course, these actions have qualifications that are pragmatic. One can interpret that killing for self-defence or out of compassion for the victim would be acceptable.

Stealing could also include trying to steal the credit or the limelight out of envy, not just a material object.

And what is considered sexual misconduct is, as we know, different in different times and different cultures. For example, living together out of wedlock could be sexual misconduct in some societies but in many cultures, it may be looked at as essential before making a lifelong commitment. It is not prescribed with 'morality' in mind.

Imagine a community in which committing crimes are the norms. Hence, Wise actions are beneficial for the greater good of the mankind.

'The best politics is right action.'—Mahatma Gandhi

In that case, we have less need to hold fear and mistrust. Think about the time when we meet people who seem to follow skilful actions. We feel inspired and safe when we interact with them. Such people make a stable and safe community.

In addition to following abstinence from the above-mentioned acts, wise action could extend itself to acting out of good intentions to spread joy and relief for many.

My friend Rekha Bajaria was the president of a social service agency in Los Angeles which offered culturally sensitive help to the South Asian community. She managed to raise the biggest funds ever for this agency during her tenure and helped it to mature from a home-spun small help centre to a well-run NGO with many essential services offered.

Why was Rekha able to raise big funds more than ever before? It is because the funders trusted her. She never tried to steal the limelight or take away what belonged to others. She worked tirelessly behind the scenes and also ensured transparency in management of funds. The community also trusted her. They felt their funds were given to the right person for the right cause.

In May 2020, when all of India went into lockdown due to the Covid-19 pandemic, Indian actor, film producer and model Sonu Sood helped thousands of stranded Indian migrant workers to reach their homes by arranging buses, trains and chartered flights. He even ensured that a chartered flight bring home 1,500 Indian students stranded in Kyrgyzstan (NDTV 24 × 7 July 2020).

'There is a saying that children close their ears to advice but open their eyes to example,' writes Sonu Sood in his memoir *I Am No Messiah*.

He launched a website and app called Pravasi Rojgar to help migrant workers find suitable jobs during the pandemic. In a society where rape, murder and robbery are sensationalised, Sood set an example, especially for people with influence and power, on the importance of acting with kindness. The sincerity of his actions has been inspirational for many.

Essentials of wise livelihood

Spiritual path is often associated with renunciation of the material world. Hence, many who desire success in their business do not follow Buddha's path. However, Buddha's advice varies for householders and monks. He does not discourage professional success. He advises against a livelihood that is based on greed, hatred or self-glory as the primary motive.

The late Subrata Roy who started with a capital of just Rs 2,000, built a business empire by collecting deposits from millions of poor and rural Indians with limited or no access to formal banking services. The cookie crumbled after the market regulator Securities and Exchange Board of India (SEBI) moved against him for alleged illegal mobilisation of funds. He was driven by greed and not by the desire to let poor people increase their savings.

The 'bad boy billionaire's' megalomania showed up in the form of extravagant display of his wealth. Money acquired from greed, lack of empathy and self-glory got him in trouble and, not surprisingly, his entire conglomerate collapsed.

On the other hand, during the thickness of the pandemic, OYO rooms chose to respond to its customers and partners with care. Their business was gravely hit due to the ban on travel. However, they ran the business with professionalism and empathy for their partners. As part of the OYO Care initiative, they partnered with 24-plus state ministries, 50-

plus hospitals and local authorities and offered some of their properties for pay per use quarantines and self-isolation facilities at affordable prices to minimise the possibility of infection and maximise social distancing and hygiene. They provided accommodation support to medical first responders at affordable prices (Oyo Rooms, official blog).

In small cities like Jamshedpur and Kota, hotel owners helped daily-wage workers and labourers by offering food packets in their property. Wise livelihood driven by compassion has allowed OYO to overcome the pandemic in spite of lay-offs and halt in travel business.

Buddha allowed room for reforms. The karma that we collect can be changed by altering our core values. King Asoka reformed from a violent expansionist to a peace-loving ruler. Bill Gates and J.D. Rockefeller evolved from money-chasing business tycoons to philanthropists. Their core values changed from cut-throat business expansion to benevolence.

All these practices are in service of being a good member of a *sangha* or community. Living according to our core values gives us meaning and purpose in life and also adds to our sense of well-being by staying relevant.

Dharma in the Bhagavad Gita

> ***'I believe that every right implies a responsibility; every opportunity, an obligation; every possession, a duty.'***
> **—J.D. Rockefeller**

Dharma from the Bhagavad Gita can be translated as our innate duty and can be interpreted as living our core values by living our purpose in life, by living what we are born for.

Swami Muktananda completed his MBA from IIM Calcutta and worked in the corporate world for three months. However, he kept contemplating and asking, *Who am I*? Eventually, he quit the corporate life and followed renunciation. After years of studying Eastern and Western philosophies, he now specialises in mind management and runs an NGO in Dallas, Texas, called JKYog.

He says that it is tough to translate dharma in English. He adds, 'Terms like righteousness, good conduct, duty, noble quality, etc., only describe an aspect of its meaning.'

He translates verse 35 from Chapter 3 in the Gita like this:

श्रेयान्स्वधर्मो विगुणः परधर्मात्स्वनुष्ठितात् ।
स्वधर्मे निधनं श्रेयः परधर्मो भयावहः ।।३५।।

'It is far better to perform one's natural prescribed duty, though tinged with faults, than to perform another's prescribed duty, though perfectly. In fact, it is preferable to die in the discharge of one's duty, than to follow the path of another, which is fraught with danger.'

This verse asks us to do our duty even if we do not do it perfectly because it gives rise to stability of mind and harmony. If we do the duty as prescribed by others or under outside influences and temptations, it is drudgery and can create unbearable stress. Prince Arjuna was tormented because he was in a war with his own uncles and cousins. The potential of killing

'No one should abandon duties because he sees defects in them. Every action, every activity, is surrounded by defects as a fire is surrounded by smoke. If you perform the sacrifice of doing your duty, you do not have to do anything else. Devoted to duty, man attains perfection.'

—Bhagavad Gita, Chapter 18, Verses 48 and 49

them did not feel right to him. However, Lord Krishna told him not to cling to such ideas that are imposed upon him because of the social conditions. He was born a warrior and his dharma was that of a warrior.

The prince is a warrior who is using his skills to correct wrongdoing. To use them to the best of his ability was his duty to himself, without getting bogged down with the results. He could still be at peace with himself in spite of the results because he was living his dharma.

As we can see, living our core values is not always easy. Dharma puts us in touch with our own purpose, hence one can say it makes us go above the mundane.

The Gita and Buddha's teachings both have influences from the ancient Indian thought. The Gita was supposedly compiled between 400 BC and 200 BC—around the time when Buddhism was a prominent force in India. Some scholars (for example K. N. Upadhyaya) believe that the Gita was influenced by the non-attachment philosophy of Buddhism.

There are some major differences in the way non-attachment is attained in the Gita and in Buddhism. In the Gita, non-attachment is achieved by surrendering our ego to the Supreme Lord and by taking action without expecting rewards. Here the permanence of the soul and self is affirmed.

On the other hand, in Buddhism the soul and God are never explicitly discussed in early teachings. To realise how everything is impermanent, including our notion of self, is a way to cultivate non-attachment in Buddhism. In both Buddhism and the Gita, non-attachment includes not clinging to greed and hatred.

Core values and well-being in the West

I went on Amazon website to check the number of books on happiness. I found 60,000 books with the word 'happiness' in their titles and subtitles. There is a reason why happiness work has become such a big industry in the West—and slowly spreading to the rest of the world. The happiness industry thrives on human craving for always wanting to be happy and feeling pleasant. Although we know in our mind that 'happy ever after' does not exist in reality, we keep looking for it. Ironically, as Buddha would have said, our attachment to happy feelings is a big source of unhappiness for us.

Thinkers, psychologists and serious happiness researchers in the West recognise that the 'pursuit of happiness' needs to be changed to 'cultivating well-being' which is attainable and makes life worth living. Happiness is the pleasant and joyful feeling we have in the moment which by nature is impermanent since survival itself requires stress. On the other hand, well-being is an overall sense of having a good life which includes happy moments and moments of unhappy feeling with the acceptance that difficult experiences could lead to meaning in life. Living life with core values is a huge part of experiencing well-being because core values add meaning and fulfilment to our life.

The following are just two examples of the emphasis on core values in the West in the well-being field.

Dr Martin Seligman, the father of positive psychology, was taking out weeds in his garden. When his five-year-old daughter tried to help him, he yelled at her for disturbing him. In her sullen voice, she reminded him that she had not whined once since she had vowed to give up whining on her fifth birthday. If she was capable of giving up whining, she reasoned, her father should be able to 'stop being such a grouch'.

This made Dr Seligman realise that as a psychologist, he needs to figure out how to be the opposite of a grouch. Thus, he started figuring out how to cultivate well-being in our lives. He researched on how to use human strengths to achieve authentic happiness and fulfilment. This opened up the field of positive psychology.

Positive psychology has a big overlap with Buddha's work, which focuses on how to reduce suffering and bring well-being in our lives and others. Just like Buddha suggested following the core values as a means to bring meaning to our lives, Seligman also suggests meaning as a pillar of well-being.

'Doing a kindness produces the single most reliable momentary increase in well-being of any exercise we have tested.'—Dr Martin Seligman

Secular Buddhist scholar Stephen Batchelor observes in his book *After Buddhism* that practising mindfulness could reinforce the selfish isolation of the self by immunising practitioners against the unsettling emotions, impulses, anxieties and doubts that assail our fragile egos.

This is *not the only thing* what we want—just to be immune ourselves. We want our practice to include spreading good in the world too. Hence, core values play an important role. Batchelor further writes in the book, 'The kind of secular Buddhism I envisage is the one that considers core values as the necessary framework for humans to flourish and to realise ultimate concerns.'

Aha! Moment

When I contemplate letting go of greed and aversion, core values emerge. For example, instead of eating a big cheesecake all by myself, I could share it with someone I care about because I realise it makes me feel good to see that person enjoying it too.

9

How to Discover, Practise, Reset And Refine Your Core Values

Let Your Core Values Be Your Guiding Light

'If you're not willing to accept the pain real values incur, don't bother going to the trouble of formulating a value statement.'

—*Harvard Business Review,* July 2002

Tata Group: the *ratan* of core values

'Culture becomes embodied in the DNA of an organization,' said Ratan Tata to an interviewer with CNBC-TV18, way back in 2017 when asked about how the Tata Group has retained a legacy of integrity, responsibility, excellence, pioneering and unity for 125 years. The core values of the Tata way of life was planted by its founders who earnestly believed that the Tata Group belonged not only to the founding family, but also to India. So strong was this investment in these core values that it drove the group to make India excel in steel production, power generation and hospitality. J.R.D. Tata exemplified humility. 'JRD would stand in line, instead of jump a queue, where he would give way to a customer first,' proudly stated Ratan Tata, former chairman of Tata Sons, in an interview on Linkedin (3 December 2018). These actions were embedded in every Tata leader spanning the next half a century.

However, the Tata values have not been immune to temptations, political pressures or shortcuts. Nano, Tata's pet project, was mired in controversy about land acquisition for the factory in Singur, West Bengal. While the state government wanted Tata to build the factory, it would have affected the livelihood of 15,000 farmers who depended on the fertile soil in Singur. In spite of initiating the construction of the plant in January 2007, Ratan Tata decided to pull out from the state after learning that 30 per cent of the land (Wikipedia) allocated to the factory was acquired from farmers without consent. The Nano factory then went on to be built in Gujarat, with the right legal approvals. It was built with the values Tata stood for—excellence and responsibility. While Ratan Tata admitted that their values had been constantly challenged by political powers or competitors, he felt most at peace when he would come back at night and say, 'I have not succumbed.'

The story of Tata's way of life is one embedded in core values and sticking by them no matter what, even if it meant dealing with errant employees—'no matter who it was, if you broke the code, you left the company'.

Want to know how you can not only identify core values, but also incorporate them as building blocks of life?

Dive deep.

How to use your core values as your guiding light

Core values hold a central place in ancient Indian teachings, referred to as *shila* in dharma (in Sanskrit) or sila in dhamma (in Pali). Buddha constantly referred to wholesome qualities (*kusala*) to be practised and unwholesome qualities (*akusala*) to be aware of. Sila and kusala collectively are called core values. Core values help us navigate towards meaning—not the type that makes us look and feel good. Meaning and purpose that need to be

- discovered,
- practised,
- reset again and again, and sometimes augmented or
- refined.

The activities, exercise and meditation technique discussed in this chapter will help achieve these.

Discovering your core values

Sometimes, we may not be aware of our core values. They need to be discovered. This may happen when we decide to take a deep dive into the well of our mind or need a guiding light during difficult times. In the eight-week-long Mindful Self-Compassion programme developed by Dr Chris Germer and Dr Kristin Neff, there is a beautiful exercise outlined to help us get in touch with our core values. We have made use of parts of the exercise here.

Activity 1: diving into a deep well

This is a written reflection exercise, so please keep a paper and pen handy. Place your hand over your heart or elsewhere, feeling the warmth of your touch, leave aside your thinking mind and get in touch with your feelings.

Imagine that you are near the end of your life, looking back on the years between now and then. Now answer the following questions:

- What gives you deep satisfaction, joy and contentment looking back at your life?
- What core values were expressed in your life that gave you meaning and satisfaction?

Remember you are thinking of a core value and not things or events. For example, if you felt joy and contentment because of mentoring an underprivileged child into a sustainable career, the underlying value could be your value and belief in equal opportunities. Please write them down.

- What makes you feel that certain actions that you undertook were not in sync with your value system?

For example, when you look back at your life you may wish that you had treated people with more consideration rather than irritation although you value being compassionate and non-judgemental.

Please write the answers down.

Identify the values that have been with you always and circle them. These are the values that you can continue practising with ease. Next, identify those values that feel out of sync or are constantly causing conflicts and worry. Circle them as values under development. You are becoming aware of what is important to you.

You have begun the process of discovering your own core values.

Activity 2: finding your way through a dark forest

There are times when we face a dilemma and need to make decisions. We may be engulfed with emotions such as guilt, shame, sadness, intense envy, extreme anger and even revenge. Difficult as it is, this is a good time to explore what our real core values are. This can not only offer us strength and solace, but also take away our fear and anger.

Imagine you are walking in a dark forest, fumbling with fear and uncertainty. Suddenly, you find that you have a matchbox in your pocket and you are able to use it to create a guiding light. You are able to now see the path that can take you out of the forest. It is still difficult, but now you have a sense of relief and direction.

The dark forest exercise is precisely designed to help you with such situations.

Step 1: Go through the exercise and see where your situation fits one or more categories in the figure.

Step 2: Circle as many core values as you see fit in that category. Add core values if they are not included in the list and they fit your situation better.

Step 3: Go through the list of the circled core values. Do they make you feel anxious, or do they give you a sense of rightness? Pick only one or two from the ones that make you feel the sense of rightness when you close your eyes and visualise yourself in a dark forest with this guiding light in your hand. If they happen to be not-so-'wholesome', but you feel good about yourself or find solace by choosing it, pick that.

This is your guiding light in the difficult situation you are handling.

Imagine you lose a competition and are feeling miserable. You can decide to either quit or work harder at the next opportunity. You may discover at that instance that either resilience or pragmatism is your core value.

Going through life's challenges can create upheaval—a divorce, a child coming out of the closet, quitting a steady job to following an unconventional career choice. If individualism is your core value, you will make unpopular life choices.

When Arin, a twenty-five-year-old, decided to take care of his old parents by moving back into their house in Nagpur from Mumbai, it meant changing his career goals and giving up an independent life. For him, caring for others and his family are his core values.

Dark Forest Exercise

Our typical difficulties in life can be divided into the five categories: behavioural pattern, relationships, finances, career and body. We can approach them with core values.

Behavioural Pattern	Relationships	Finances	Career/ Work	Body
Commitment Curiosity Diligence Future generations Humility Humour Justice Nature Non-harming Openness Optimism Patience Resourcefulness Respect	Adaptability Beauty Belonging Caring Compassion Family Forgiveness Generosity Gratitude Harmony Honesty Loyalty Self-compassion Trust	Abundance Courage Generosity Giving back Independence Security Status	Achievement Being the best Health Integrity Responsibility Service Success Teamwork	Beauty Health Peak Performance Self-care

Source: Authors

Aha! Moment

'Core values have the potential to take my fear and anger away.'

Practising your core values

Practising our core values could be difficult even when we experience solace from them. Mindfully becoming aware of the difficulties that come in our way and coming to terms with them is the next big step. The difficulties cannot be just shoed away always by using willpower. Sometimes, we need to look at them with compassion and wisdom.

Activity 3: working on the roadblocks

Consider a situation in which you are having a hard time living according to your core value.

For example, your core value is taking care of the family, but you have health issues preventing you from being there for your family. You may feel guilty or irritable or self-pity arising from this situation. This may manifest in unpredictable ways and may even become more detrimental to your health.

Think about why you are unable to live according to your core value.

Sometimes the limitations come from external reasons—such as health issues or financial problems or other obligations demanding your time.

Many a time your own psychological make-up may come in your way. In the above example, you may be harbouring resentment for the demands on your time by family and that may be too much for you to handle especially when you have health issues popping up. Other internal blocks could include fear of failure, internal self-criticism, tendency to overanalyse and being indecisive.

Now close your eyes and place your hand on your heart. Be kind to yourself instead of either blaming or pitying yourself. Ask these questions to yourself:

- Is there anything I can do to make the situation better for me and others?
- Can I remove the internal obstacle(s) by any means?
- How do I invest in my spiritual development, or take professional help, or share with close people or rightfully communicate with people involved?
- Can I remove the external obstacle(s) by any means?

Now comes the important part. If you are unable to remove the impediments right away, accept the difficulty of the situation. Offer a lot of compassion towards yourself. The work lies in coming to terms with the hurdles being there and not to fight them.

Like Dr Germer would say in his workshops: 'Whisper to yourself in your ears, "I forgive you".'

Resetting your core values

Unfortunately, none of us is perfect. And that is why resetting our core values is critical. 'Falling off the wagon' is not a good way to describe when we end up not living with core values because that is part of the process of learning. If this happens, we need to remind ourselves what our core values are and then reset them by going back to living with them. Buddha's teachings have many suggestions for how to handle distracting thoughts when we are trying to focus on what we want, a wholesome quality, a core value. We have the following suggestions based on these teachings modified to suit our modern times.

Say, staying calm in the face of chaos is our core value, but we have our own triggers, which make us lose our cool often. This is a right time to reset. This leads us to the next activity.

Activity 4: replaying and resetting

Play the unpleasant situation in your mind, which made you explode. What made you react that way? Depending on your temperament, you may choose one of the approaches from the list below or change approaches to see which one works based on the situation reviewed in hindsight.

Self-compassionate approach

Remind yourself that there was a reason why you exploded. Remember that you care about your own core values. Forgive yourself and think about the situation again in your mind with a good response. Calm and effective, the way you wish it would be.

Thoughtful approach

Slow down and pay attention to what exactly happened that stopped you from being calm. What was the trigger? Giving a good thought to the trigger may help to reframe it. You exploded or reacted involuntarily because you had already explained the issue, but the person did not pay attention. *Was it frustrating?* Take a few deep breaths to slow down in the moment. You could remind yourself that this person perhaps did not like the demanding voice you had used and hence did not pay attention. Since you want that task to be done, you need to use an inviting voice, as opposed to a demanding voice the next time. A good reason to live with your core value: effectiveness and a delayed reaction.

Trigger the unpleasant

You can associate unpleasant memories with your explosion or ineffective reaction. A fight from the past that was hard to bear. The visceral response of tummy churning and throat choking. A wax figure melting like your calmness did. Allow such images to be associated with the explosion. Next time you feel the same explosive reaction, a visceral feeling may show up first and if you are mindful of that feeling, it would be a signal to switch your approach away from explosion, away from an ineffective reaction.

Willpower

When recreating the situation in your mind, pay attention to the moment just before the explosion. Remember how that felt. Again, and again. Each time tell yourself to *stop*. No other thoughts and considerations in the moments. Just *stop*. Leave the room if you need to. You can handle it better after removing yourself from the situation.

Activity 5: managing conflicting core values

One of the characteristics of core values is that they can be conflicting. And the conflict always seems to arise as soon as you have decided your core value and the right way forward. This is the universe's way of testing us. There can be various ways, for example:

A promotion and a raise for your co-worker as soon as you have decided to quit your job for your passion.

Friends organising a party on the day you have decided to quit sugar and prioritise well-being.

A fight with your fiancé on your wedding day about the decor when you had decided months back to keep it a green and sustainable wedding.

Meditation 1: Resolving the Conflict of Core Values

1. Decide to do this meditation until you are calm and relaxed, no matter how long it can take. Resist the urge to escape from uncomfortable feelings, conflicts and thoughts in the middle of the meditation.
2. Close your eyes, with spinal cord straight.
3. Allow the breath to have its normal pace and notice how the body is receiving it. Here and now, in this moment.
4. Identify the conflicts arising from your core values.
5. Resist mixing them up and focus on the most persistent one.
6. Look at the options you have in front of you based on how your core values are being tested. For example, mental well-being and family are your core values, but you are unhappy in your marriage. Do you stay or separate amicably?
7. a. Visualise Option 1 (i.e., stay) and see how that feels in your mind and body. Notice your breath, thoughts and feelings.

   b. Visualise Option 2 (i.e., separate) and see how that feels in your mind and body. Notice your breath, thoughts and feelings.
8. Stay with each of the sensations for as long as you can until there is clarity on which option makes you calm, comfortable and relaxed.
9. Take a few deep breaths before letting go of this meditation.
10. Repeat this meditation every time a conflict occurs.

Refining your core values

It is also important to note that core values sometimes need to be changed or augmented based on changing demands from changing times. Younger generation now expects more positive reinforcement as opposed to criticism. This may require parents, educators and employers to change their core values to empathy from tough love. At the same time, career options are more non-linear and passion-driven in today's time. This may require us to view earnings as a potential S-curve instead of an elevated slant.

Regardless, core values are constantly evolving and as long as we are aware of this, we will be able to discover, practise and reset them.

Aha! Moment

My core value is like my mentor. She always cares about my well-being and guides me through tough times. However, there may come a time to say goodbye to her because my needs change. It may be a fight or an amicable break-up, but it is always after a lot of contemplation! Not a frivolous jump from one to the other.

SECTION 5
Compassion

10

Why Practise Compassion?

An Age-Old Path to Well-Being

'If you want others to be happy, practise compassion. If you want to be happy, practise compassion.'

—His Holiness, the fourteenth Dalai Lama

Compassion in a crisis

In 2015, when the AirAsia plane Flight QZ 8501 carrying 162 people disappeared near Indonesia, its CEO Tony Fernandes wrote on Twitter: 'This is my worst nightmare.' But he did not hide behind his desk. In a few hours, he was in Surabaya, speaking with families of the crew and the passengers.

And when the remains of the flight were found in the coastal Indonesian town of Pangkalan Bun, Fernandes was there in person. At the same time, AirAsia was issuing regular updates about the known facts in several languages and had set up a hotline for relatives.

Fernandes described it as a 'soul destroying' experience to see the bodies and the airplane debris being pulled out of the water. This approach is in sharp contrast to that of Malaysian Airlines, which quickly became the nation's heavily indebted flag carrier after having two fatal accidents owing to miscommunication.

Being at the site with grieving families made investors react more positively to the crisis AirAsia was facing. Zulkifli Hamzah, the head of research at Amanah Investment Bank Berhad, speaking to AirAsia's investors, said confidently, 'I don't think this will break them. I think the main thing right now is to protect their brand, and I think that will be instrumental in the future of their company.'

Tony was not only the first to arrive at the location of the accident, but also changed AirAsia's bright red logo into a sombre grey one to reflect the state of the passengers' families. Fernandes has made sure that the single, first fatal accident did not make it synonymous with the brand. Some may say that the compassion was shown for keeping the brand image. Even so, this shows that feeling compassion is an appeasing feeling in the face of a tragedy and many leaders do not recognise that.

AirAsia's ethos of being led by a CEO who believes in a hands-on philosophy with accountability reflects on how the crisis was handled with utmost compassion. Fernandes acquired the airline at a token sum of one Malaysian Ringgit or 29 cents. In 13 years, he turned AirAsia from a state-owned airline with millions of dollars in debt to Asia's largest budget carrier.

As he built the brand, Fernandes became synonymous with the airline, becoming the chief promoter, sometimes working alongside cabin crew or at reservation desks or even as a bag handler (*Business Standard*, 15 May 2024).

Understanding compassion

Buddha was believed to have said that compassion was one of the core values to live by. But before making it one of our core values, we must understand its intricacies. It is also important to accept the limitations of compassion in our lives and to practise it at our own pace. Then it can have the power of creating joy and meaning. This chapter is intended to take you deeper into that understanding.

Compassion is often not completely understood. We may think of it as caring for others in pain. Sometimes we believe that compassion is the same as empathy. Or that compassion means to always see the other person's perspective. In reality, compassion is much more than that.

We tend to think that compassion means to be sugary sweet to everyone and never to use any unpleasant words. A compassionate employer cannot fire an employee even when they are incompetent. A compassionate parent means they never get angry with the child.

People have resistance towards exercising compassion because they think it will make them weak, a pushover or a doormat. This misconception keeps us away from experiencing the power of compassion.

Let us dive deep into understanding the nuances of compassion with openness.

> ***'Compassion is an attitude that not only wishes for others to be free from suffering but is also associated with commitment, responsibility and respect towards others.'***
>
> **—Dalai Lama**

Compassion is all of the following:

- It is empathy and a genuine wish to reduce suffering in others.

- This empathy is not us sinking in the flood of our own emotions, but a recognition of pain. We need to have the ability to be open to suffering without falling apart, i.e., non-attachment.
- It is based on the understanding of common humanity that we all experience suffering and we want well-being, that is, Law of Dependent Origin. We are all connected and affect each other.
- We need commitment to compassion. However, we may not want to rely on the feelings of the moment. Making compassion our core value will allow us to align it with our decision-making.

Compassion can be 'cruel' too

'Compassion is, by definition, relational. Compassion literally means "to suffer with", which implies a basic mutuality in the experience of suffering. The emotion of compassion springs from the recognition that the human experience is imperfect.'

—Dr Kristin Neff, pioneer in compassion research

Compassion can be cruel too. Although in layman's terms, compassion is the caring and loving feeling we have when we see someone suffering, in Buddha's world, it is not just a feeling.

It is a sense of responsibility we have in reducing suffering. Sometimes this means that compassion may seem cruel because we are acting out of care and out of well-being and not just to 'look good'. A teacher who uses harsh words to impart good habits in a pupil is acting out of compassion.

An employer who fires a person because they do not fit into a role might benefit the employee in the long run because they will start looking for appropriate alternatives. In fact, by keeping the employee in the job in which they would be facing disappointments would go against the act of compassion.

One can say that this is an act of cruel compassion. If the firing is done with anger, malice and an uncaring attitude, the employee would be traumatised. This is clearly not an act of compassion. As someone rightly said, 'Honesty without compassion is cruelty.'

Compassion is *not* a weakness

Compassion has an important component: self-compassion.

This implies that the way we want the suffering to be reduced for others, we want suffering to be reduced for ourselves too. In order to feel good for others, it helps to have our own bucket of wishes filled too. Otherwise, while expressing compassion for others we may feel either resentful or anxious.

Self-care with care for others is a balancing act. When balanced properly, it can provide us with the power to handle difficult situations without feeling stressed.

The irritated cabbie

I remember being upset with a rude cab driver who was unhappy about the remote place where he needed to drop us off. My co-traveller, Nitesh Batra, was a trained compassion teacher who seemed so calm that I noticed the contrast between his reactions and mine.

Finally, when we were dropped off, he handled the cab driver's agitation so empathetically and calmly that the cab driver also seemed to have calmed down. We safely reached where we needed to go. I realised that my getting worked up and saying harsh words to the cabbie really would have served no purpose.

Was Nitesh being weak in this instance? Quite the opposite. He was so composed that the conflict dissolved.

Why to practise compassion with non-attachment?

The bird of mindfulness has two wings—non-attachment and compassion. Both wings need to be strong and balanced at the same time for this bird to fly well. Non-attachment can give us the non-clinging and non-reactive focus, but without compassion being just as strong we could use this focus for becoming a bank robber! On the other hand, just being high on compassion without the psychological distance allowed by non-attachment can make us into a person who throws rational solutions out of the window because of too much compassion.

It is a balance of the heart and the head. Non-attachment helps us to create the appropriate distance from attachment and pain, and compassion helps us to turn towards pain with a sincere wish to reduce it.

How much is too much compassion?

'My problem is that I have too much compassion! I cry every time I see someone suffering. What do I do with that?' One student asked me many years ago when I had begun teaching mindfulness. I have heard it frequently since then.

This is called over-identification: to mix up our experiences with someone else's. This is exactly why we need to cultivate non-attachment through mindfulness practices because it reminds us that each person has their own journey to follow.

If we see a wound in another person's arm and if our arm starts hurting, it simply means mirror neurons are probably firing to motivate us to help the wounded person. Our arm is *not* their arm. If we fall apart ourselves, we are unable to help.

Over-identification can lead to another problem—imposing our solutions on another person.

Imposing well-being is not compassion

I had a client who volunteered for an NGO that worked with victims of domestic violence. My client got extremely angry and disturbed with the woman, whom she was helping to make a life away from her husband, when she went back to him. My client could not sleep for a couple of nights. She was ready to disown this woman.

'Have compassion for everyone you meet, even if they don't want it.
What seems conceit, bad manners or cynicism is always a sign of things no ears have heard, no eyes have seen.
You do not know what wars are going on down there where the spirit meets the bone.'
—Miller Williams

We had conversations about being compassionate but simultaneously to be mindful of the victim having her own journey and to respect that. My client chose to keep in touch with the woman and to listen to her. Eventually, the woman was ready to leave her husband and received truly compassionate help from my client to look for the right shelter and right training to become independent.

In the movie *Maja Ma*, Madhuri Dixit's daughter is an LGBTQ activist. She accidently finds out that her traditional housewife mother is a lesbian. The fiery daughter then badgers her mother to come out of the closet and be free. She is so invested in giving this freedom to her mother that she takes her mother to a LGBTQ centre under another pretext to meet a counsellor.

To the daughter's immense frustration, the counsellor says that the choice of coming out has to be the mother's. She should not be forced into it by anyone else. Forcing her out could have disastrous consequences. When the mother finds such freedom as her core value, she would be ready to face whatever difficulties arise.

So, good intensions are not enough. We need to have a good judgement of what can help the person's needs, not what we want them to have.

The benefit of practising compassion as a core value

According to Buddha's teachings, compassion is not just a feeling which comes and goes, it is a core value. This means that we do it as our guiding light irrespective of the consequences.

This allows us to find meaning and purpose in our helpful act. It can be a truly joyful feeling to extend ourselves to others and to see them adding ease in their lives

It is difficult to feel positive towards anyone acting out of arrogance, selfishness or harmful intentions.

'There is no way I would have compassion towards someone who hurts my child! I would want them to rot in prison and burn in hell,' one very tough woman said in my compassion class.

She is not among the minority. Most of us will have a hard time feeling compassion towards someone who has unfairly and brutally hurt us or our loved ones. This is because we mix up compassion with feeling of love, which it is not. The right way to think about it is exemplified by Osama bin Laden's death.

Killing Osama bin Laden

When Osama bin Laden was killed, Dalai Lama implied that it was justified to kill him. Many were surprised that the messenger of peace and compassion would approve of killing instead of forgiving a person.

Later Dalai Lama clarified that there is a need to find a distinction between the action and the actor. He said bin Laden's actions were destructive, as the terror committed on 11 September 2001 killed thousands of people. So, his action must be brought to justice. However, we must have compassion and a sense of concern. His Holiness said therefore the countermeasure, no matter what form it takes, has to be compassionate action.

'Forgiveness doesn't mean forget what happened … If something is serious and it is necessary to take countermeasures, you have to take countermeasures.'—Dalai Lama, *Los Angeles*

Times, 4 May 2011

This suggests that the harmful action was stopped, even when we may have an understanding of the perpetrator's own struggles. This is an example of cruel compassion.

Thus, exercising compassion is not always possible to do seamlessly and therefore, if we acknowledge that it is a journey, we will be open to practising a life of compassion.

Sometimes, our negative reactions and self-preservation may come in the way of having compassion towards an evil person. Buddha advises to watch these feelings without acting on them immediately. Insights may arise and then, we would know what the right action is for us.

For example, the mother who claimed that she would want the person who harms her kids to burn in hell, may get an insight when she visits the person in prison more than once and communicates her angry feelings to the person in order to find closure for herself.

Keep on the journey of living with the core value of compassion even when we may have to struggle with some situations and then we will see how it offers refuge from fear, hatred and many other negative experiences.

Aha! Moment

Planting seeds of compassion in my mind's soil makes way for tree of life. This tree of life will offer solace of its shade and the nourishment from the fruits. But for the tree of life to grow healthy, I need to nourish it with the sunshine of self-compassion and the rains of non-attachment.

11

How to Cultivate Compassion towards Others, Self And Negative Emotions

Understanding the Critical Pillars of a Good Relationship

> 'The dark thought, the shame, the malice, meet them at the door laughing, and invite them in. Be grateful for whoever comes, because each has been sent as a guide from beyond.'
>
> —Rumi

The mother-in-law dilemma

Rita was infuriated at her mother-in-law for taking her son's side which left Rita handling all the guests alone while her husband happily went off to a networking dinner at work. This was the last straw on the camel's back.

Her mother-in-law (MIL) would often dole out unsolicited advice to Rita about her relationship with her husband, as if she knew the eternal truths. That day, Rita argued and fought with her MIL who got defensive and sarcastic at the same time, which made Rita all the more frustrated.

She ended up saying they needed to take a break from the argument and left the room. She even considered taking a break from her marriage. This was in the early stages of Rita's mindfulness training. She decided to sit in meditation and allow herself to observe her anger with non-attachment. And let all feelings and thoughts arise in her mind without suppressing.

Rita observed all the thoughts arising with a gusto first and then slowly. The feelings manifested in her body either as a burning sensation or a throbbing headache. She watched the images and associations that were showing up. And as she was watching them, she calmed down and realised how she too had created harm by using harsh words.

At first, her mind defended her own actions, and then she had an epiphany. She felt compassion for her MIL and herself. She could see how anger hid hurt, fear and frustration for both of them. She realised how her MIL valued their relationship and expressed it in many ways like cooking hot rotis for her or stitching the lost buttons on her kurtis. She thought to herself, *Just like I wanted to be seen and understood, so did she. Just like I defended my hurtful actions, she did too.*

Once she understood the hurts and longings underneath the anger, Rita felt sad instead of angry. She was now able to handle her resentment differently. More often than not, she handled the preachiness with humour or simply learned to let go. Since the MIL noticed a change in Rita's reactions, her attitude changed too. Eventually, they started communicating with each other and understanding each other's actions, minimising friction.

Months later, Rita adopted this method to improve her relationship with her husband as well even though they never really had any pressing issues. They both attended a weekend-long couple's compassion workshop. They did an exercise in which they were asked to imagine their partners as little kids.

At the end of the exercise, Rita's husband shared with the group, 'As a little girl with a lot of dreams, it must have been hard to make the dreams come true. As a woman, Rita had to work much harder and endure more disappointments. I feel so much compassion for her now.'

Rita was surprised to hear this and very touched. He was not the type to wear his heart on his sleeves or say things lightly. This was another milestone in their relationship.

Compassion as a critical component of a fulfilling relationship

Feeling a sense of connection with someone close gives us satisfaction. Connection is felt when we share something mutually with another human—love, humour, interests, feelings, points of view or, sometimes, even a painful experience.

Our pain becomes bearable when the other person understands it in a deep way. We have basic needs to be understood, heard or seen by another person. We long for a sense of belonging somewhere and with at least a few other human beings. It makes us feel safe. Being completely accepted by another person despite our flaws and past mistakes is a blessing. When we feel such a connection, we feel many heart-warming and positive emotions like joy, excitement, bliss, safety and courage.

Feeling disconnected from people we care about is a difficult thing to bear. Certain negative emotions like anger, envy, guilt, shame, sadness, fear, disappointment and anxiety lead to disconnection.

Relationships with our partners, parents, children, close friends can lead to either joy or pain. Relationships are the greatest source of joy and pain. Conflicts are inevitable in all relationships.

There is one critical element to sustain a fulfilling relationship—compassion.

Commitment and communication are two known pillars of a good relationship. However, we often do not realise that without compassion, the pillars can shake. We need all three Cs—commitment, communication and compassion—for sustaining any close relationship.

To make relationships thrive, we need to have compassion for people and compassion towards our negative emotions.

Compassion towards people

A fellow meditation teacher once told us how his relationship with his mother had changed after he started training for compassion. He had a difficult relationship with her, so every time his mother tried to talk to him, he would feel irritable and this reflected in his tone.

He had no patience to listen to her complaints against his father or other relatives. However, after his training in loving kindness compassion meditations (more on this later), he found himself saying the following in his mind for her. *Mother, may you be happy. May you be safe. May you be at ease. May your troubles be reduced.* And gradually his irritation melted away and was replaced with compassion.

When he realised that his mother needed to get all her angst out in front of him because she felt it was a safe place, he listened to her with much more patience and even offered some validating words like 'I see what you are saying'. Sincere and genuine compassion for people is to recognise that others too want to reduce their discomfort and increase joy, just the way we want it for ourselves.

Don't forget self-compassion

In one of my seminars on relationships and mindfulness, one woman came up to me and said, 'It's all fine but if I have empathy for my husband, he will just take me for granted. For example, I make tea for him every morning and he happily sips it while reading the newspaper. But it never occurs to him that I may want him to make tea for me too sometimes. I too enjoy reading a newspaper and sipping on my tea.'

She had a point.

One-sided compassion may make us feel like a doormat. The answer is to balance compassion with self-compassion. As Dr Neff says, 'Self-compassion would mean to treat ourselves with kindness the way we would treat our best friend.' Acknowledging that we have needs by not sweeping them under the rug is self-compassion. The next step is to *communicate* those needs to people who matter, with compassion. For example, the woman in the above example could ask her husband to make tea for her on Sundays. Also, she needs to reflect if she is serving tea to her husband because she likes to make him feel comfortable or because she feels obligated. Her action and communication would depend on recognising her own core values and having confidence in them. This too is self-compassion.

Self-compassion does not come naturally to us because many of us are used to being tough on ourselves. Because we believe that if we are kind to ourselves, we will become complacent and thus not 'improve'. However, research shows that motivating ourselves with kindness is more effective than self-flagellating. The good news is that cultivating self-compassion is possible with practice.

However, compassion towards others and ourselves needs patience and meditation. When it comes to relationships, it needs to be combined with communication as well. Communicating our needs is just as important as understanding other's. This is when the other core value of 'wise speech' would be useful.

Compassion towards negative emotions

A way to practise compassion towards negative emotions within the mindfulness framework is to re-examine the way we treat our negative emotions.

We are naturally aversive to unpleasant experiences. A way to befriend the negative emotions is to practise non-attachment and compassion towards them. Non-attachment suggests *not* to react to negative emotions right away but to practise non-reactivity and observe.

Treating negative emotions with compassion would mean to understand that they have a purpose for existing. They all bring some message to us to keep us safe. We don't want to miss out on that message because it may give us some valuable perspective.

Unless we understand the importance of being unhappy (with compassion), difficulties keep their status quo and keep showing up in the same way again and again. Instead of jumping to feeling pleasantness, if we face unhappy emotions the way I have suggested below, it has a huge potential to make us mentally strong and happy.

Anger

Anger is a secondary response to our primary emotions of fear, hurt or frustration. Anger as a response to these primary emotions makes us feel powerful, as opposed to weak and vulnerable.

Although the Buddhist way of resolving anger is to completely let go of it, we must acknowledge that there are times when the power expressed by anger indeed is an effective way to get things done. If we want the message to be conveyed quickly and with emphasis, anger can be more effective than cajoling. An angry customer gets their way more than a nice one. Anger is useful when we wish to break up with or create a distance from someone. It makes us say things honestly that otherwise we may not say because of the fear of hurting the other person's feelings.

However, if we value a relationship and wish to sustain it, know that anger is an emotion that creates distance and pushes people away. It is a poison that we drink wishing that it would kill the other. It helps to pause and think about why we are feeling angry. What are we afraid of? Do we feel hurt? Do we feel frustrated? Our anger is bringing us this information which may not always be obvious unless we contemplate over it. This information can change our impulsive angry response to a constructive one.

For example, if you are angry that your friend is rude and you are tempted to just yell at her to butt out. Upon reflection you may realise that you are hurt by what you perceive as disrespect, but you really value her opinion. You would much rather have her give you her feedback, but only if you ask for it. It may be more effective to tell this to her honestly rather than pouring anger upon her and silence her.

The antidote to angry feelings against someone who is close to us is to take a pause, be patient and reassess the conflict with compassion for the person. Think about their battles. If we can relate to any of their wishes to want joy and harmony, we have reached a good place. If we approach the person with this, the conversation changes, like in Rita's story.

Pema Chodron beautifully explains the antidote of patience against anger in an article in the magazine *Lion's Roar:* 'Patience means getting smart; you stop and wait. You also have to shut up because if you say anything it's going to come out aggressive, even if you say, I love you.'After getting smart with patience, we may get insight into what right action we want to take. Then we take that action. *This is where delaying reaction becomes powerful.*

Envy

In the Ramayana, Kaikeyee's envy of Kausalya's son, Ram, inheriting the throne of Ayodhya led to banishment of Ram and Sita from the kingdom for fourteen years. This had long-term and widespread repercussions for many. Envy is when someone else gets something that we have always wanted.

If our neighbour buys an expensive car or our competitor at work gets the promotion that we felt we deserved, we may feel envious. If we allow envy to get hold of us, it can create destruction. But envy can be turned into inspiration if we use the right antidote.

Ever thought why most people are envious of their neighbour who is more prosperous but not of Bill Gates? Envy informs us that we have potential in us, ready to be cultivated further. If we have no singing talent, we will not feel envious of a good singer.

If we still feel envious of a singer, it may be because of the attention they receive from their singing, implying that we have some need and potential for getting such attention. If we see many happy photos of friends on social media when we are feeling low, we may feel envious because we want to feel happy ourselves.

In fact, envy can bring us the message of our greatest wish and our potential. It could inspire us to find ways to get what we desire. Someone who craves fame could decide to explore their own talent and get inspired to foster it to a level that can get them attention.

An effective antidote to envy is to practise sympathetic joy or *mudita* in Pali and Sanskrit. Sympathetic joy is to experience happiness for other person's good fortune by separating our story from theirs. In the book *Loving Kindness*, Sharon Salzburg writes that happiness is not a limited resource and by sharing the joy of another person, we are not depleting this resource. If we allow ourselves to genuinely feel happy for someone else, the difficulties felt because of envy goes down and positive feelings arise.

This positivity makes us open to receive the message of inspiration and work on it. Imagine Kaikeyee experiencing sympathetic joy towards Ram's mother. This would have changed an enormously negative impact on the lives of many. Could she have got inspired to create something else, as powerful, for her son Bharat?

> ***'Achieve some perfection yourself, so that you may not fall into sorrow by seeing the perfection in others.'***
>
> **—Rumi**

However, it is not natural and easy to feel sympathetic joy unless we intentionally work towards allowing happiness to arise in us when we hear about someone else's good fortune. There are specific meditations for cultivating this habit.

A study published in the *Journal of Social and Personal Relationships* says that if you experience sympathetic joy when your partner feels positive emotions, it greatly benefits the relationship. This benefit is greater than empathy expressed for negative experiences of the partner. Just as it helps to be there for the partner in difficult times, it helps even more to be their cheerleader.

Jealousy

'Mirror, mirror on the wall, who is the fairest of them all?' asked the queen.

'Snow White.'

The queen flew into a fit of rage.

> ***'It is not love that is blind, but jealousy.'***
> **—Lawrence Durell**

So far, the mirror had always answered, 'You, of course, my queen, is the fairest of them all.' But now Snow White was snatching away that coveted position of being 'the fairest of them all' from the queen. In a fit of jealousy, the queen tried to poison Snow White to get rid of her once and for all.

Jealousy is to feel threatened that someone else is taking away what is ours and valued. A common example is to be jealous when we perceive that our romantic partner is paying romantic attention to someone else, if we believe that such attention is mine and only mine.

Evolutionary psychologists say that jealousy exists because it can motivate us to work hard on keeping what we fear we may be losing and save it from being stolen away from us. If it is in the context of a relationship, it is a wake-up call that we need to pay more attention to the relationship. Jealousy brings us a message about our insecurity. This can be a painful feeling, but it helps to know that everyone has some insecurities, sometimes very hidden and it helps to unearth them and then to heal from them.

How would it have been if the queen had understood her own insecurity that aging was making her lose her 'fairest' looks and to come to terms with the fact that we all age? Acceptance and non-attachment to 'me, mine and my ideas' would have helped her to age gracefully. It might have been possible to cultivate other qualities that may help her to feel good about herself—maybe charity, kindness, mentoring young aspiring princesses?

Antidote to jealousy is radical acceptance, instead of fighting with the situation and defending ourselves. With non-attachment, we learn to accept the moment exactly the way it is instead of being hijacked by the hatred for the person who made us feel jealous. Recognising and coming to terms with our insecurity, gives us an opportunity to process it and decide our next course of action. It may give us the freedom to notice the positive experiences that we may be overlooking. Or it may point to the direction that we need to leave the situation in order to heal from our insecurities. Or it may open us up to a completely different set of experiences.

Shame and guilt

> ***'My guiding principle is this: guilt is never to be doubted.'***
>
> **—Franz Kafka**

Shame is when we believe something is wrong with us and guilt is when we believe what we did was wrong.

Dr Germer, co-founder of the Centre for Mindful Self-Compassion, describes shame as an innocent emotion we feel when we want to be loved. When we are ashamed, it is because we feel we will not get approval from others. For example, we are ashamed of being a shy and a quiet person in a boisterous party where we believe we would get sneers from others. Understanding shame in this specific case would mean to mindfully be kind to ourselves and remind us that we are loved for our other qualities (for example, thoughtfulness) and not just based on our ability to be boisterous or a stand-up comedian. The antidote for shame is practising self-compassion. Self-compassion work may need to be accompanied by other therapy modes if the shame is based on a traumatic event. Shame can be ingrained and hard to shake if the root cause is trauma-based.

Guilt on the other hand is if we do something wrong. If we have chronic feelings of guilt, it can turn into shame. Know the feeling 'something is wrong with me'? Guilt brings us a message that one of our core values is broken. It is a good reminder of what the core value is.

If we feel guilty about yelling at the shopkeeper for not bringing the promised groceries for three days, our core value may be staying calm or being respectful. We could remind ourselves to stay calm and in control the next time a similar irritation sweeps over us. Guilt can inspire us to return to living according to our core values and therefore, that is the best antidote to guilt.

Disappointment

Researcher Brené Brown says, 'Disappointment is unmet expectations and the more significant the expectations, the more significant the disappointment.' In any relationship, we have expectations. When we are disappointed, it informs us about our expectations. The expectations are often from our primary needs of being seen, heard and understood.

> ***'Trying to design the perfect plan is the perfect recipe for disappointment.'***
> **—Patrick Lencioni**

On top of it, there could be the need for self-recognition; to be respected, to be valued, sometimes even narcissistic need for special attention—towards me, mine and my ideas. We are social animals and we want our needs to be met by others around us. Regardless, disappointment in a relationship can lead to so much heartache. But there is good news too, if we are willing to patiently introspect.

Disappointment gives us a chance to examine our expectations. Upon introspection, we may realise that our primary expectations are not being met in the relationship. If these basic needs are unmet, it is helpful to have self-compassion and see our own needs clearly and with kindness. It helps to see and understand us in order to even consider how to get them met.

Although not relying on anyone else to meet our needs and to become completely self-sufficient may sound like a good plan, living in a community may make it hard to achieve it perfectly. As a result, managing disappointments is a dance between self-sufficiency and communication, non-attachment and self-compassion.

If we care about our relationship with a person, we may want to view their disappointing behaviour with compassion. They too may have an unmet expectation. Or our reaction to our disappointment may be creating suffering for them too. We may realise that our expectations from the person are unfair.

If parents are expecting their child to become a doctor instead of pursuing their passion, it may not be right to insist that the child study medicine.

Sometimes, we need to make a choice between leaving the situation where we experience disappointment versus staying and doing the dance. In such cases, reminding ourselves of our core values helps us to make a decision. If parents are disappointed because their son is getting married to a girl from a different religion, they may have to remind themselves of their core value of family. Is it a strong value? In that case, they are choosing to do the dance between non-attachment and self-compassion instead of disowning the son. On the other hand, if a wife is disappointed because the husband is unwilling to accept that his alcoholism is leading to an adverse effect on kids, the same core value of family would finally allow her to leave the husband after years of suffering or forcefully coax him to go to a rehabilitation centre.

Anxiety

Stress is part of our modern life. In fact, some stress is good because it helps us to tighten our belt and get things done. However, too much stress can be paralysing but the ability to experience the present moment in mindfulness allows us to let go of it. Anxiety is the fear of something we are expecting to happen in the future. It is as what we dread not happening right now. Worry is thoughts out of the anxiety that keep arising in our mind.

Stress and anxiety both can be detrimental to any relationship. Stress stops us from paying attention to others and focuses on getting things done. Anxiety can be truly debilitating if it stops us from noticing the positive aspects of a relationship or our own success because we are busy fearing the future.

Anxiety increases our negativity bias, which means that we latch on to negative experiences and then draw conclusions about people and future based on that, with the hope that it would prepare us for the future. We can imagine how this would adversely affect relationships that are close to us.

More often than not, anxiety informs us that we are holding on to a banana which is making us imprisoned. Issues around body image, finances, relationships and self image are the typical bananas we hold on to when it is more than just wanting—it is a craving that traps us.

> ***'Our anxiety does not empty tomorrow of its sorrows, but only empties today of its strengths.'***
>
> **—C.H. Spurgeon**

Clinging to our banana(s) may affect our relationships. For example, if we are so chronically worried about losing weight, it affects our mood, which affects the mood of everyone around (banana: body).

Our obsession about reaching a certain financial status, affects our ability to enjoy small things like a family visit to a restaurant (banana: finances or self-image).

Our anxiety over perceiving that we may be on the streets because of losing our job may be making us unhappy and rude to those close to us(banana: finances).

Our constant vigilance over our partner treating us exactly the way we believe is 'respect and love' may stop us from noticing and enjoying what is already working in our relationship(banana: relationship).

A father's anxiety over his son turning out to be as 'manly and sportsmanly' like him may become a source of conflict between him and his sensitive and effusive son (banana: self-image).

The person who is experiencing anxiety never questions its validity. The only way we can recognise our banana is an honest introspection when we are mired in anxiety. It helps to talk it out with someone we trust or a therapist.

It can be surprising to know that our desire can give rise to anxiety. Once we admit what our banana is, we can remind ourselves to let go of it at least for the moment whenever we feel trapped. And then see how it feels. We have a certain image of how life needs to look like for us to be okay. If the banana is a relationship, as we let go of it, it becomes easier to feel calm.

If we are open to a different image emerging, the anxiety can be managed. We can call this Plan B. Being fine with Plan B adds so much comfort to our lives.

Plan B for the person suffering from a chronic health condition could be to find an activity where they can get so engrossed that it can offer them meaning. A person who is obsessively worried about reaching a certain financial status, the Plan B could be to be surrounded with well-wishers who appreciate their current status.

The over-vigilant partner may choose Plan B as noticing and cherishing their partner's love language. A father who is anxious to make a sporty man out of his son may choose Plan B as appreciating whatever his son chooses without getting into self-destruction.

This table below summarises the messages brought to us by negative emotions that carry useful information for contemplation, and the antidotes we could use to resolve them constructively.

Negative emotion	Message to ponder over	Antidote
Anger	What is my fear, or hurt or frustration underneath the anger?	Patience and reassessment with compassion.
Envy	What is my wish and how can I get inspired to realise my own potential?	Sympathetic joy.
Jealousy	What is my unresolved insecurity? How do I heal from it?	Radical acceptance before deciding the action, mindfully noticing the positive experiences.
Guilt	Which core value of mine is getting violated?	Vow to living according to our core value as much as possible.
Shame	I want to be loved and approved. How can I soothe myself?	Showing self-compassion.
Disappointment	What are my unmet expectations?	Practising self-compassion, or compassion. Core value to tell when to apply which one of the two.
Anxiety	What is my banana?	Let go of the banana. Compassion. Allow Plan B to be present.

Source: Swati Desai

Try this exercise

Step 1: Understand compassionately the message from the emotion(s) and let it sink in.

Step 2: Apply the antidote to resolve the negative feelings constructively.

Step 3: Only after this, choose to turn towards the positive feelings the way it suits you.

To transmute pain into joy, we first need to get the message pain brings us and then use the right antidote. Antidotes don't always come to us naturally but they can be cultivated with practice. And it comes with practising the four aspects of mindfulness.

'The most important lesson that man can learn from life is not that there is pain in this world but that it is possible for him to transmute it into joy.'—Rabindranath Tagore

Aha! Moment

Applying antidotes to difficult emotions is not a natural thing for me but it can be cultivated.

But it is worth it because with antidotes, I will be able to float, swim and maybe even miraculously walk over turbulent waters of life.

12

The Art of Close Relationships

Managing through Mindfulness

'Buddha went looking for an answer to reduce suffering from three inevitable things that happen in human life: ageing, illness and death. He forgot to add the fourth inevitable suffering that happens in human life—relationships!'

—Chris Germer, the co-founder of the Center for Mindful Self-Compassion

How to deal with problematic relationships

Close relationships, as connecting and fulfilling as they can be, are also the source of conflicts, heartburns and empty buckets of ice cream. These are relationships we have with parents, children and close friends, and since these are important relationships we like to sustain them and try our best to salvage them.

'Hell is other people,' French existentialist Jean-Paul Sartre famously said in one of his finest plays *No Exit*. If a relationship is twisted, interaction with the other person can be a hellish experience. How do we untwist our problematic relationships?

As a psychotherapist who has counselled people on relationships, parental and romantic, etc., I can say with confidence that there is one essential ingredient to sustaining a relationship—compassion.

The rubber meets the road especially when it comes to close relationships. We need compassion as the driver and the other two Cs, commitment and communication, as passengers. With the other aspects of mindfulness (present-moment awareness, non-attachment, core values) working as accelerator or brakes, relationships can be transformed into a meaningful ride.

But wait, an important thing needs to be understood. The lubricants and water needed to sustain this vehicle are diligence and patience.

Let me share my client's account of how he dealt with conflict in his relationship with his spouse.

Stage 1: acknowledging the raw expression

My wife and I were hosting few friends. She was making fun of my parenting style and I had no comeback. Again! This made my blood boil. She had the annoying habit of bringing up sensitive issues in front of friends.

The fact is that I feel extremely angry when my teenage daughter wants to attend parties, which I am not okay with but my wife is. We have had many fights over this in front of our daughter. I have many a time reasoned with my wife along the following lines:

'This is ridiculous. I am bewildered at your bad judgement. Our daughter is just fifteen. You know what happens in these parties. You want her to get into drinking and boys? How can you be okay with this? This is the time to make sure we instil good values in her to avoid future problems. And how could you just oppose me in front of her? You think you are a better parent than me? You need to look at yourself in the mirror. You like to control everything and go opposite of what I want. That's the only truth. Sometimes you just amaze me!'

My wife protests. She thinks that it is better to let our daughter do things that her peer group is doing and be open with us. Because if we stop her, she will start hiding from us. I simply do not agree. We fight. We take out old wounds. We accuse each other. My wife has a hard time keeping quiet when I am angry.

She thinks I am attacking her, and hence she becomes agitated and explodes. We end up not talking to each other for a few days after a fight except over routine matters. I do not allow my daughter to attend the party. My wife becomes even more silent. In the end, she brings up the issue again to defend her actions.

'Why can't you tell me in plain language, what is on your mind, without getting angry? You start assuming that all I want is control. But you don't listen to me. You just explode. Maybe this is why I bring it up in front of friends so that you cannot explode. Have you thought about that? Your anger is very hard to take.'

As she talks, she becomes agitated again. Her voice quivers as if she is about to cry. It is then when I start feeling guilty but manipulated. So, I don't give up. It ends up with my wife saying, 'You have an anger issue and push me away because of that. You need to communicate better.'

'You don't want to admit you are wrong. You only want to defend yourself and push the blame on my anger,' I reply.

Most situations start with a raw expression screaming in anger or completely stonewalling each other. This causes both parties to remain stuck in their own positions. The person who faces anger follows their own fight, freeze or flight reaction. Some fight back with more anger. Some suppress their anger and don't express it at all and freeze positive feelings too. Some people get emotionally pushed away when they encounter anger and exercise flight. Then they get back with a passive hurtful action such as lashing out about an unrelated aspect.

Stage 2: adding compassion, slowly but surely

In my mindfulness practice, I chose compassion as my guiding light. My goal was to do effective problem solving.

I chose to have compassion in my heart for my wife. My practice helped me understand that she expressed anger because she felt hurt too. She felts hurt because she thought I did not hear her out. Instead, I stayed stuck to my point and got livid. This is thc rcason why shc says what shc wants in front of our friends.

When I put my own side aside, I can see why she did that. I feel less angry with her. I bring up this issue again in front of her.

'I know we both have good intentions for our daughter. Let us see how we can make it work. I really don't want you to ambush me by bringing it up in front of other people. That's what makes me irate. I know why you want to give permission to our daughter to go to the party. So, this time I will let that happen.'

But I am still having a hard time admitting that my anger may be too much to handle because I feel justified. I also am still a bit angry about being ambushed. My wife senses this but doesn't know what to do. She keeps being reserved but she is relieved that I am meeting her halfway.

At least we had a cordial conversation. We agreed to let my daughter go to the party but have some rules in place such as no alcohol and curfew time. We agreed that we will revisit the rules in the future depending on what comes out of it this time.

This particular time it worked; however, patterns don't go away overnight.

I had a nagging feeling that I was the one giving up too much and my wife had begun to expect it. She was not appreciative of my changed approach. From my side, I was battling with the question: 'What about *me*? I need compassion too!'

How did I deal with this?

Stage 3: practising the 'must-have' self-compassion

Compassion towards others must also include compassion towards myself. Without self-confidence and self-worth, compassion towards others can create resentment.

Replacing insecurity with self-compassion helped me to be open to having compassion towards my wife as my core value, regardless of what came back to me, and also confidence in what my needs were. I know that I do not like to be ambushed but I also know that I needed to communicate without exploding. We were both having our difficulties. Now I have empathy for both of us. This view changed my experience.

Stage 4: practising non-attachment

I know that mindfulness practice emphasises on watching without sinking or clinging, in other words, non-attachment.

I practised non-reactivity by creating space between me and my emotions when they became too much to handle. I just watched when I became overwhelmed—with distance.

This helped me to see how my brain made stories when I was angry. I painted my dear wife as a proud and uncaring monster who was only interested in getting what she wanted. I forgot that she gave a lot of attention to my needs.

She was not clingy and was obliging whenever I asked her for help with something—be it mediating in a dispute in the family or getting things done around the house. Most importantly, she was not malicious.

Stage 5: creating distance from distress in the present moment

To create distance from distress, I noticed the distress in my body. I realised the importance of knowing how the present moment showed signs on my body. I allowed the distress to be around and learned to tolerate the negative feelings in my body. Eventually, I felt transcended. In fact, I realised what a superpower it was to not let negativity be expressed outside of the body but to welcome it to stay. It went away eventually. Then I decided what to say and when.

Stage 6: living with my core values

Cultivating compassion as my core value helped tremendously to exercise it even when there were no immediate results. I imagined my wife as a little girl and my heart filled up with empathy for all the struggles she had to go through as a woman to get the career she had. I exercised my other core value—wise speech.

I decided to make a point not to communicate with anger but to explain things to her with both our interests in mind? I let it stay on my mind for some time to make it clear to me that my compassion for her was genuine and what I believed I needed from her was genuine too.

I brought up the issue with her again:

'Look, I really want us to understand each other better. So, let's try to listen to each other first and then tell what we want. From my side, I get it that my anger pushes you away. It doesn't feel safe to talk to me and hence, you end up discussing sensitive and private issues in front of our friends. I am really going to try to listen and then we can meet halfway. So, I hope you know that is my sincere wish.

'We love each other and we can make it work. From my side, I want you to understand that I am sensitive to how you treat me in public. It doesn't make me feel good even when you are saying something in jest. Let us leave that for our private discussion. Let us be mindful of each other's feelings.'

We talked about it and I watched my tone during the whole discussion because I did not want to hurt her. Instead, my intention was to bring her in. She could feel it. She agreed with me. She appreciated my efforts to listen to her. She wanted to try to be sensitive to me too.

She asked me what happens if we slip sometimes. How do we then handle it? We ended up deciding a signalling method (for example, rubbing the tip of the nose*)* when one of us slips. And talk about it afterwards instead of suppressing it or exploding.

We still slip and we argue, but soon the connection returns, and most importantly, laughter is back in our lives. We still do feel resentful and angry from time to time, but our fondness for each other bounces back much quicker.

There is a sense of safety in our relationship. We feel accepted by each other in spite of our shortcomings. Nothing can compare with this feeling of intimacy.

Let me conclude the chapter on a lighter note by quoting Henry Youngman:

'We were married for better or worse. I couldn't have done better, and she couldn't have done worse.'

Aha! Moment

Practising compassion brings me comfort and keeps me calm. When I am lost and need to find the strength to move in a direction, practising self-compassion helps reset my mind and delay reaction.

13

How to Practise Compassion

Transitioning from an 'All-Head' Approach to Life into a More 'Heart-Based' View

'Be kind, for everyone you meet is fighting a harder battle.'

—Plato

Learning to peacefully co-exist

I grew up with an extreme aversion to reptiles. Thankfully, I grew up in a city, without that much exposure to them, unlike the non-urban parts of India. I used to literally get the shivers whenever I had an occasional sighting of lizards. Many people I knew had that aversion too.

When I went for my first vipassana retreat in Hyderabad many years ago, I was terrified to find out that a little lizard had entered my room. When I requested the caretaker of the property to shoo it away, she not only did so but also said, 'You are here to get rid of fears, including that of harmless lizards!'

I smiled and thought to myself, *No chance*! *Cannot imagine that happening.*

Another time, when I was in a retreat in New Mexico on a hilltop wooded area, there were many small non-poisonous garden snakes. We had to walk to our cottages from the paths carved in the grass. I used to be so worried and averse to the thought of a possible garden snake wiggling in the grass on the side that I was petrified every time I walked back to the cottage.

When I told our teacher Dr Germer about my phobia of snakes, he said, 'I wonder if this fear could be genetic. You grew up in India with so many poisonous snakes around. Your ancestors probably had to be vigilant of them.'

That was an interesting thought. I had never seen it that way.

Years passed by. When we moved back to India to live on the campus of the Indian School of Business in Hyderabad, our apartment in the high-rise building on campus was not supposed to have any non-humans showing up. But lo and behold, one night, I suddenly encountered a little lizard frantically running on the floor.

My reaction to it was instinctively screaming as if there was a crocodile in my room. The little lizard stopped for a few seconds and looked at me. Just for a few seconds and then scurried to the corner where I stored my laundry. In my petrified state of mind, a very unfamiliar thought emerged: *What cute eyes. That baby lizard. Aww*!

As I was calling the caretakers of the apartment to come and take the lizard out, I could not believe that I was smiling at the thought of the little one with its small tail and cute eyes.

When the caretaker showed up, I told him to make sure that he does not kill Lizzy (I had already given it a nickname) and to release it.

The campus we lived on was built outside the city about twenty years ago. The terrain was known for having poisonous snakes. In the early years whenever I would visit the campus, I would be terrified of snakes, as if their sole task was to wait in hiding for me and attack me as soon as I made a wrong move. But that feeling has changed over the years.

Now I have become comfortable with the idea of peacefully co-existing with snakes. I can picture them in my mind or look at their pictures with curiosity. Although I am still afraid of snakes, I am able to walk on a path (if I have to) knowing that there could be snakes in the vicinity. To comfort myself, I often say, 'Snakes are shy. They would much rather keep away from humans. It is only if we step on them, they will respond by biting.'

My mindfulness practice has changed my 'all-head' approach to life into a more 'heart-based' view towards living beings. They too want to exist and do what they are born to do. This compassion had grown in me slowly as I became more mindful of myself and those around me (including reptiles!).

Compassion practice has also changed my marriage into a deeper connection. It has improved my relationships with my extended family and friends, has helped me feel the comfort of gratitude and has made me aware of the suffering and distress we all want to reduce. It has made me more courageous and a social risk taker.

In this chapter, I offer specific meditations and exercises for incorporating compassion into our daily life.

When we do them, sometimes it may feel mechanical. But without our conscious knowledge, the exercises change us from inside. If we remember that these practices must include self-compassion, they save us from self-doubt.

Activity 1: Practising compassion phrases

There are times when you feel distressed or a bit lost. If that happens, close your eyes and repeat compassion phrases for yourself or others whose well-being is on your mind. Compassion is the wish to reduce suffering. So, a compassion phrase is the following.

May I be free from suffering
or
May ______ be free from suffering

You may have something more specific in mind which you can use to create a phrase. For example:

May ____ find the strength to manage the difficulties.
May _____ find the courage.

It is important to note that a compassion phrase is neither a prayer (asking the higher power to grant your wish) nor a positive confirmation ('I am strong', 'I am courageous'). The intention is to warm our heart with hope and to allow us to focus on resolving the issue at hand.

Compassion phrases bring us solace if we keep practising them over a period of time, especially the compassion meditations. We learn to focus on compassion completely. Our brains begin to associate comfort and calmness from hearing the compassion phrases. This alone helps us have the right mind to find resources and peace, and to delay reactivity.

Meditation 1: compassion meditation

Practise this formal meditation as many times as you can. It may not speak to many in the beginning. However, research shows that seven weeks of compassion meditation training, one hour a week, increased the connectedness people felt and improved their immune system.

Meditation 1: Compassion Meditation

Sit in a calm place without distractions and with your back straight.

1. Close your eyes and relax your body. Get in a comfortable position. Take a few deep breaths—slowly and be mindful of the energy they bring to us.
2. In front of your mind's eyes, bring the image of yourself and send compassion phrases to yourself. Repeat for a couple of minutes.
3. In front of your mind's eyes, bring the image of a benefactor or a mentor you have had who has made a difference in your life and repeat the compassion phrases to them for a couple of minutes.
4. In front of your mind's eyes, bring the image of a loved one, someone whose well-being is important to you and repeat the compassion phrases to them for a couple of minutes. Pick one person (or animal) at a time and send them the phrases.

5. In front of your mind's eyes, bring the image of a person towards whom you have neutral feelings (for example, an acquaintance or someone whom you have noticed as a service person) and repeat the compassion phrases to them for a couple of minutes.
6. In front of your mind's eyes, bring the image of someone who has been difficult in your life and repeat the compassion phrases to them for a couple of minutes. This is going to be a difficult part for most meditators. Be gentle with yourself and let it go if you are unable to do it. Just remember, if the difficult person suffers less, it is more likely to reflect in them being good to the world—including to yourself. Alternatively, you may want to use a phrase: 'May this person find compassion for themselves and others.'

Meditation 2: let the body remember

Buddha (and the new science of interoception) says that all experiences are felt in the body—a lot of times without our conscious knowledge. In our meditations on mindfulness of the body sensations, feelings and thoughts, we practise cultivating this awareness. This type of awareness of the body during an experience of an emotion can enhance our familiarity with that emotion.

For example, when we feel compassion towards someone, we may feel a comfortable warm feeling in our tummy along with sadness experienced in the form of tingling in the head. It is different from when we feel only love for someone, which may generate only the warmth in the tummy. Paying attention to how our body feels compassion affirms compassion in a deeper way.

The science of interoception says that our emotions are felt in the body first and then our brain interprets what these sensations mean to us ('Interoception: the Hidden Sense That Shapes Wellbeing', the *Guardian*, 15 August 2021). Knowing this helps to regulate our emotions by checking if our brain's interpretation of our body sensations is to catastrophise or downplay (depending on our nature and nurture). When we are feeling overwhelmed or annoyed, we could purposefully allow compassion to be felt in the body. This will make our brain get the signal to feel safer and optimistic. Compassion, after all, is an antidote for anger, disappointment and anxiety.

The following meditation will help you understand this.

Meditation 2: Let the Body Remember

1. Sit comfortably. Take a few deep breaths and feel the energy coming in the body.
2. Inhale and say to yourself, 'I breathe in compassion.' Exhale and say, 'I breathe out compassion.' Repeat this to yourself for a few minutes and attempt to focus on feeling compassion for someone who you believe needs it. This may be you yourself.
3. Now pay attention to the body and examine how it feels when you are breathing compassion in and out. Allow yourself to be filled up with compassion and watch the body until you feel something in the body.
4. Pay close attention to the body and try to remember how compassion manifests itself in the body.
5. Do this for as much time as you wish to.

Activity 2: compassionate listening

Picture this. You are under distress and your heart is heavy. You talk to a person who is close to you and cares about you. When you feel that the listener understands your pain and validates your experience, you feel a sense of relief. Your processing of those feelings becomes a bit lighter.

On the other hand, imagine you are pouring your heart out to someone who is constantly distracted by phone calls or WhatsApp messages, or interrupts you with 'Oh I know—let me tell you my story…', or tries to tell you how your thinking is wrong before even understanding your side of the story, or offers you unsolicited advice like: 'All you need is self-confidence. Believe in your own capability and everything will be fine.'

This can leave you feeling even worse than before. This is not compassionate listening.

Compassionate listening would be to

1. listen with open heart and carefully,

2. withhold negative judgements about the person's story and try to see their side first,

3. give complete attention without getting distracted,

4. avoid the temptation to interrupt with narration of your own story and taking the spotlight away to yourself and

5. try not to provide advice unless asked for or offer it with permission.

When I ask my students to do the compassionate listening exercise with each other, most are pleasantly surprised. The storyteller feels relief. The listener feels good about giving something valuable to the other person. This practice with friends and family can be healing for all.

However, if it is a spouse or a partner or a close friend, compassionate listening feels more difficult especially if they complain about us. Try the following. Keep your own feelings aside for a moment and do compassionate listening. Then ask the person to reciprocate the gesture. If judgements and anger surface, talk about them.

Remember that intention and impact are two different things. If our good intentions have the impact of hurting others, first we can apologise for hurting them instead of defending ourselves (which is very annoying!). Then, we can explain our good intentions. This practice can change the relationship dynamics; however, it will require resetting again and again because slipping is inevitable.

Activity 3: looking around

When you are performing your daily activities like walking, working or running errands, look around. You may notice other people or animals or birds. You may also notice people walking or driving with anxious expressions on their faces. Or even people haggling or manipulating others. Understand that they too want well-being for themselves just the way you want.

Although their ways to achieve that may be different from yours, they too desire happiness, respect, love, safety and more for themselves. Regardless of how we are on the outside, each one of us is fighting our own battles internally. Even animals and birds want to be safe and do their own things. To recognise this is the beginning of our journey into compassion.

Activity 4: practising loving kindness phrases

Loving kindness is a goodwill wish. The way compassion is a wish for reducing suffering when a person is under distress, loving kindness is to wish happiness and well-being for a person regardless of their predicament. Regardless of whether their success comes in your way or not. In fact, when we care about someone, we want them to sustain their happiness and good fortune. Traditional loving kindness phrases are:

May ____ be happy.
May _____ be safe from physical and emotional harm.
May _____ be at ease.

We can come up with our own loving kindness phrases such as:

May ___ sustain their happiness.
May ____ find good fortune.
May ____ find success in their endeavour.

We can cultivate the habit of sending loving kindness phrases to people we care about. In fact, it helps to send such phrases to people with whom we are not comfortable. Our discomfort may be reduced by recognising that they too would like to find some solace.

Sometimes, people we love and care about can make us uncomfortable too. Our parents, children, close friends, co-workers or even bosses—may say things that are hurtful. Or there may be a conflict due to disagreements. If we care about this relationship, it is healing to send loving kindness phrases to them. It can help us to get in touch with what we appreciate about them.

Just like compassion, it helps to practise loving kindness in a meditation form, as it will enable us to experience the warmth when we need it in daily life.

Meditation 3: loving kindness meditation

This meditation is the same as the compassion meditation except the phrases are loving kindness phrases. Both the meditations may be combined into loving kindness compassion meditation by using both types of phrases one after the other.

Meditation 3: Loving Kindness Meditation

1. Close your eyes and relax your body. Get in a comfortable position. Take a few deep breaths—slowly and being mindful of the energy they bring to us.
2. In front of your mind's eyes, bring the image of yourself and send loving kindness phrases to you. Repeat for a couple of minutes.
3. In front of your mind's eyes, bring the image of a benefactor or mentor you have had who has made a difference in your life and repeat the loving kindness phrases to them for a couple of minutes.
4. In front of your mind's eyes, bring the image of a loved one, someone whose well-being is important to you and repeat the loving kindness phrases to them for a couple of minutes. Pick one person (or animal) at a time and send them the phrases.

5. In front of your mind's eyes, bring the image of a person towards whom you have neutral feelings (for example, an acquaintance) and repeat the loving kindness phrases to them for a couple of minutes.

6. In front of your mind's eyes, bring the image of someone who has been difficult in your life and repeat the loving kindness phrases to them for a couple of minutes. This is going to be a difficult part for most meditators. Be gentle with yourself and let it go if you are not able to do it. Just remember, the loving kindness to others is your value as opposed to a momentary feeling. This makes it possible to send goodwill wishes to difficult people. Alternatively, you may want to use a phrase like this: 'May we both find happiness and well-being.'

Activity 5: examining judgements that counter compassion (live and let live)

Our brains are made to judge because we want to protect ourselves by judging 'unsafe people'. However, very often, we judge out of fear even when the person may not pose any danger to us. It could be because we are afraid of losing our emotional safety because the person thinks and behaves differently.

Sometimes, it gives us a feeling of superiority to judge others and connects us to another person with the same judgement. The problem with taking our own judgements too seriously and acting on them is that: *it could create a type of violence against the person.* Even when it is benign, it stops us from feeling compassion towards the individual. This can push people away and can make us feel lonely or angry or both. And of course, a mind that judges others is also judging themselves harshly. These are the times when judging is, in fact, making us emotionally unsafe. It serves us well to cultivate a habit of not taking our judgements at face value. Mindfulness practice is about observing things non-judgementally.

The exercise helps us with this.

When you find yourself judging others, ask yourself, 'Is the behaviour intentionally meant to harm me or people?' And if the answer is 'not really', say to yourself, 'They too want good things for themselves, just like me.'

Let us go through the various scenarios to understand this better.

From a distance

When you find yourself judging a person in a party, ask yourself, 'Is it harming me?' If the answer is 'not really', withdraw the judgement.

For example, if you are judging the person for being overweight or wearing unfashionable clothes or having an annoying voice, say to yourself, 'They too want good things for themselves, just like me.'

From close by

When someone close to you behaves in ways different from yours and you find yourself judging them, ask yourself, 'Is it harming me?' If the answer is 'not really', withdraw your judgement.

For example, if your friends' parenting style is different from yours or your friends have a habit of showing off their wealth or your sister posts 'too much' on social media, say to yourself, 'They too want good things for themselves, just like me.'

If the behaviour is harmful to you

Let's say the answer to the question, 'Is it harming me?' is 'Yes', then reflect in what way(s). Is it harming the attachment to 'me, mine and my ideas?', then think if it is possible to leave it alone? For example, if your friend's taste is tacky and hence, you don't want to be seen with them, it may be attachment to 'me (my image)'.

If your friend's habit of asking you to borrow your things when you are unable to say 'no' makes you judge them as 'takers', it may be attachment to 'mine'. If your relative supports gay marriages and you don't, it may be attachment to 'my ideas'.

In such cases, ask the question again, 'Is it really harming me?' Check if it is possible to let it go by saying to yourself, 'They too want good things for themselves, just like me.'

If the harm feels real, it is beyond judgement. Then it is time to take some action.

If the behaviour is harmful to others

Say, the answer to the question 'Is it harming me?' is 'Not me but maybe others', then see if it is really your business. For example, you may judge your friend's partner as short-tempered. But your friend seems to manage it. Then your judgement may be hurting your friend, hence it is better to leave it alone. Say to yourself, 'They too want good things for themselves, just like me.'

However, if it is harming someone who has no power to avert it, it may require taking action. It may not be just a judgement. For example, if a friend has an anger issue that is manifested in emotional or physical violence against their family, it demands some appropriate action.

When a situation demands action because it is spreading harm, we want to think about action to take—not out of passion of the moment—but compassion towards the ones affected by the harm. This type of compassion can be referred to as 'fierce compassion'.

Meditation 4: practising sympathetic joy (antidote to envy)

As we cultivate compassion towards our habits producing unhappiness, we can let the feelings be there and see what they are teaching us. Then, we can work to use an antidote to create happiness. For example, the antidote for envy is to take inspiration from whatever we are envious about and then feel genuinely happy for the person with good fortune.

The meditation for sympathetic joy can be divided into two parts. Each part can be practised on its own or together. Doing these meditations will greatly alter our unhappiness.

Meditation 4: Practice Sympathetic Joy

Part 1: Contemplation over the Inspiration

1. Close your eyes and take a few deep breaths to pay attention to how the energy is coming in the body in the present moment.
2. Allow the feelings of envy come in the mind. Think about what exactly you would like to have for yourself from the good fortune. Once you know what you want, contemplate over if there is way for you go towards achieving it. Once you know the direction you could take, the burden of envy may be lifted a bit.

Part 2: Experiencing Sympathetic Joy

Close your eyes and take a few deep breaths to pay attention to how the energy is coming in the body in the present moment.

Allow the picture of the person you are envious of or the situation that is making you envious to come to your mind's eyes.

Looking at this, say to yourself, 'I join in your happiness.' Allow the joy to be felt in the body. Send it to the person or the situation.

If the joy does not feel sincere, just acknowledge that. Know that joy is not a limited resource that gets exhausted by giving it to someone else. Your joy is independent of sending joy to others.

It may be difficult to send joy to the person if you believe the person is arrogant or undeserving or has made your life difficult. Watch this distress with compassion for yourself. Say to yourself, 'I am struggling with this.'

See if it is possible to practise the sympathetic joy for the person as your own core value, independent of the character of the person. There is an advantage for you in this of setting a good intention.

If there is difficulty in experiencing joy for the person, try saying to yourself, 'May I find my own good fortune too. Let us both have our own joyous moments.'

Once your heart is filled up with joy for you both, you can stop. If not, promise to yourself that you would try it again and then stop.

Activity 6: using the antidote to anger

Taking a pause when anger arises is exceedingly difficult. As you try to cultivate this ability, you will often slip and have your usual autopilot anger response. Whenever that happens, look back at anger in this way.

Anger is like fireworks consisting of a medley of colours. But underneath it, there are some specific colours—blue, orange or red each representing hurt, frustration or fear, respectively, the real reasons that get expressed as anger.

Now allow yourself to experience the white colour—calmness and patience—the antidote to anger. See if your heartbeats slow down. With calmness now think about what you would like to do the next time you feel infuriated. Contemplate over that.

Meditation 5: mindfulness of anger

This meditation can be done for controlling anger and the thought associated with it. This may offer us insight into what action we may want to take in response to anger.

Meditation 5: Mindfulness of Anger

1. Close your eyes and take a few deep breaths to pay attention to how the energy is coming in your body in the present moment.
2. Reflect on the incident when you felt anger come to your mind. Allow the anger to arise if it feels safe. Watch the anger.
3. Create a distance from the anger and watch the mental images, the colours, the thoughts and the body sensations that arise. Mind will wander around a lot but keep bringing it back to watching all these phenomena arising because of anger.
4. Try to identify the underlying emotion—hurt, fear or frustration. Allow that to float around in your mind. Observe what arises.
5. Keep compassion in mind. Each one of us wants the same thing—respect, validation and love.

6. You may get an insight into the right action to take to control your anger. If not, let it be. No need to do anything until such an insight arises in you. Wait for the next time when you get a chance to do this meditation again.

Using your body for emotional regulation

The new field of interoception research says that our body feels the sensations first and then our brain interprets them based on our previously stored experiences. Buddha too had given body the primary importance in choosing how we react to experiences.

So, when someone insults us and if we feel our heart pounding and head throbbing, our brain may interpret it as anger if we have had prior experience of such sensations. Hence, if we train ourselves to pay attention to our body sensations and choose to interpret them as neutral or safe, it may train us to be equanimous to potential aggravation. It may turn us into compassionate individuals, full of our loving kindness. And our job as authors would be fulfilled when another episode of fireworks occurs and you respond differently!

Aha! Moment

Practising compassion will change my experience of the world into more empathic and less harsh. This is where the peace of mind comes from.

SECTION 6

Mindfulness in Real Life

14

Acing Parenting

How to Apply Mindfulness Irrespective of Your Parenting Style

'Parenting is about raising and celebrating the child you have, not the child you thought you'd have.'

—Brene Brown

While writing this book, as mothers, we realised that mindfulness can be practised in parenting no matter one's age, nationality or stage. In today's age of social media, there is extreme pressure on parents to be perfect—gentle with boundaries, worldly yet traditional, financially aware but not spoilt. The list is endless, pressure is immense but the solutions seem confusing. Good news is that mindfulness can be practised in parenting without complying to a parenting style. Now that we have understood the four aspects of mindfulness, it will only equip and enable one to be a better parent.

Let us see how the four aspects of mindfulness can come together and be practised in the life of a parent.

We are parents, we are humans.

In a world that is so quick to tweet a judgement and post a reel on best parenting tips, we often forget that parents can make mistakes and are meant to learn from them. The jargon seems endless on how parents are categorised.

Tiger moms are those strict mothers, heavily invested in their child and pushing them to attain high levels of academic achievement. Penguin dads are nurturers, ones who go beyond the norm and rock a baby to sleep or tie their daughter's hair or choose to extend paternity leave in support of their partner.

And then, comes the helicopter parent who gets all the flak for being overly involved and micro-managing because it is the only way they know to overcompensate for a miserable childhood.

Here, I refrain from all sorts of labelling and categorising of parents; not even the use of the most popular parenting among millennials and Gen Z—gentle parenting.

I do not intend to suggest any specific parenting style or advice on how to raise children. As a parent, you may already have a parenting style. What I intend to do is to suggest how different aspects of mindfulness could add ease, enjoyment and wisdom while you are parenting.

Hence, this chapter is about mindfulness *in* parenting, not *about* mindful parenting.

'As children develop, their brains "mirror" their parent's brain. In other words, the parent's own growth and development or lack of those, impacts the child's brain. As parents become more aware and emotionally healthy, their children reap the rewards and move towards health as well.' Dr Daniel Siegel, author of *The Whole-Brain Child.*

Dr Siegel is the founder of the Mindful Awareness Research Center (MARC) at UCLA, a child psychiatrist, an author and a parent. His quote is a motivation for parents to increase self-awareness and keep learning about themselves. Hence, this chapter focuses on the parents' mental health and not on child development.

We are both parents. While my children are grown-ups leading their independent lives, Subhashini's children are still young and need direct nurturing. Different phases and different emphasis. This chapter is about our personal experience with mindfulness in parenting and from my work with clients, again to add ease, joy and wisdom to parenting. Here's how to practise mindfulness in parenting.

Experience the joy of PNS moments

In spite of the frenzy of parenting, there are moments that are special and beautiful. These could include when a child says something special and innocent, learns to walk or code, sings or dances well in a party, shares your passion for sports or gardening, enjoys playing a board game with you or cooking together—the list can go on.

Even a teenager sometimes can come and cry on your shoulder and express closeness. Sometimes, you hear from a friend about something special the child did in front of them that you may have taught them and they may have resisted in front of you. Such moments need to be noticed deliberately and etched in memory. Otherwise, they can pass by and be forgotten.

Pause, notice and savour!

Enjoy parenting through PNS moments by completely being present in the moment and knowing that you have that moment regardless of what the future holds. As you know, the cornerstone of mindfulness training is to learn present-moment awareness as the moment is happening.

Instead of making parenting full of stress, worry and guilt, allow PNS moments to help you to relax and experience the joy.

I personally wish that I had learnt the PNS moments early in my parenting. It would have helped me to be more cheerful in spite of juggling very young kids with a career in the US and without any family help. Fortunately, as I trained into mindfulness, I became increasingly aware of the importance of PNS.

I also realised that the more you learn to do mindfulness activities and meditations, the more is the increase in your capacity to be present and enjoy the moment. The worry about the future does not interfere as much.

A comparing parent is an unhappy one

Comparison is a normal part of life but mostly takes us to a road full of unhappiness.

Don't we all know about feeling envious of other kids who may seem better mannered or more talented or more fortunate to land the opportunities in life that we want for our kids? When we compare, we put burden on ourselves and our kids that is unhealthy and unnecessary. Fortunately, I realised that the role of envy is to get inspired in the right way in order to direct my energies in a gentle and unburdened way. By practising sympathetic joy. And not being desperate.

For some parents, comparison leads to feeling superior. This is even more dangerous than simple envy. This generates false grandiosity, which is hurtful to others and sets such parents up for an eventual collapse when the child may not perform the way they desire. Taking 'self' too seriously is asking for hurt that leads to nothing but more hurt.

For some parents, comparison leads to inferiority or even self-pity. If the child is differently challenged, this could be inevitable. Cultivating self-compassion could be an enormous task and life-changing. If you are one of those parents, we bet that you are doing the best you can in spite of the limitations life brings.

But you can choose to befriend yourself with compassion instead of turning into your own enemy. Accepting your limitations with kindness and humility is self-compassion. Self-compassion is one of the key ingredients to run the marathon called parenting, without collapsing.

Always come back to the core values

Keeping in touch with our core values, in turn, puts us in touch with what parenting means to us. When we are having difficulties with parenting, we can remind ourselves of our core values. This can settle dilemmas and guilt.

I (Subhashini) am raising young kids and I believe in gentle parenting. There are times when I find myself losing my temper and saying things that make me feel guilty afterwards. After I learnt about core values, my negative feeling of guilt turned into a reminder of my core value of gentle parenting. This gave me the strength to be more mindful the next time when I find myself tempted to lose my temper.

At the same time, compassion is my core value too. This allows me to accept that some periods are more stressful than others and those are the times when I may be more on the edge. It is true when they say you can't pour from an empty cup. Compassion and core values fill my cup when I feel empty inside.

In my house, we have this sign in the middle of the drawing room as a reminder of what our core values are. While these values are unique to my parenting style, it has definitely helped me centre my feelings during a toddler tantrum, lopsided parenting duties, picky eating episodes and most recently, 'eye-rolls'!

If all else fails, maybe a sign like this in your home re-affirming core values unique to you can help navigate the roller-coaster ride of parenting. The sign in my home says:

In this house, we are real. We make mistakes. We say, 'I'm Sorry'. We are crazy. We are silly and have lots of fun. We give lots of hugs. And second chances. We forgive and laugh a lot. We love each other and have respect for WE ARE FAMILY!'

Practising our core values as a parent gives us the strength to enforce certain values in our kids and become a role model for our kids when they grow up.

Self-exploration is the key

Dr Siegel says that an important factor that decides if the kid grows up to have a secure attachment is if the parent's ability to be aware and self-reflective.

For example, say, you have an anger issue and explode any time anything goes wrong. Say, you become aware that this is not good for the kids to feel safe and at ease. Upon self-reflection you may realise that your own father had this issue and it had made you move away from your father, but you retained the anger habit unknowingly. Maybe you never learnt another way to express yourself. This uncomfortable discovery may allow you to change the old habit slowly.

Changing habits can be difficult but just the awareness of the habit results into better relationships. Mindfulness, as we know, is an exercise in cultivating awareness.

Accept growth is beautiful

Who said growing up is all pretty and positive? However, parents tend to forget them when it is their children's turn. Add to that the changing times and changing ways to express the pain. For our parents' and grandparents' times, banging doors and saying 'I hate you' may have been unimaginable. However, Gen Z are known to be expressive.

We exercise our choice by either exploding because we think it is 'entitlement' or finding support groups of parents who have similar concerns. We may want our grown children to be physically close to us and protected but the growing child may want to explore the world.

We may believe in enforcing certain rules for when and whom to get married to but our child may end up marrying someone from a different community or nationality. For us to accept the sexual fluidity that the current generation seemingly feels free to explore may be unthinkable, let alone the idea of getting a divorce.

If we want to make 'growing up' into a beautiful journey of self-explorations, in spite of the growing pains for our children, practise non-attachment slowly as our children start growing up into teens and older. Allow full engagement in their lives by accepting who they are and letting go of the craving to 'own' them.

As parents, we believe that we know what is best for the child and sometimes, we worry about the social implications of their behaviour away from the norm. Practising non-attachment to 'me, mine and my ideas' allows us to help our children when and if they want and accept with humility that we may not know enough about the world they find themselves in. The most seemingly benign and dangerous attachment is to try to impose help on the children when they are going through anything painful.

In a *New York Times* article titled 'The Harsh Realm of Gentle Parenting', Jessica Winter summarises the dilemma of parenting beautifully: 'The essential enigma of parenting, though, is that you are responsible for your children and yet you can't possibly be responsible for them. They are clay in your hands; they are the rocks that break your hands.'

The two laws of non-attachment apply perfectly to parenting. Nothing is permanent and every phenomenon depends on a chain of actions and perceptions that lead to its existence and identity. We and our child are not the same and are evolving every day of the year. And, parenting with our best efforts is only one of the ingredients under our control.

Conclusion

Practise, practise and practise all four aspects of mindfulness.

Sahil Bloom, investor, content creator, entrepreneur, has a background in sociology from Stanford University. The data he shared in late 2022 on how much time we spend with children and how much time we spend alone is inspiring and depressing at the same time.

Time Spent With Children

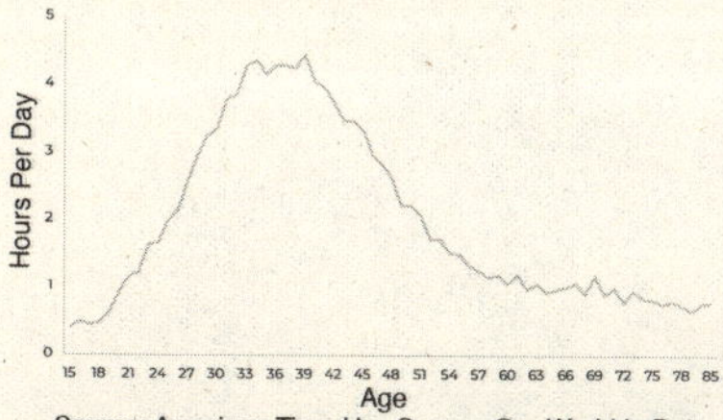

Source: American Time Use Survey, Our World in Data

Time Spent Alone

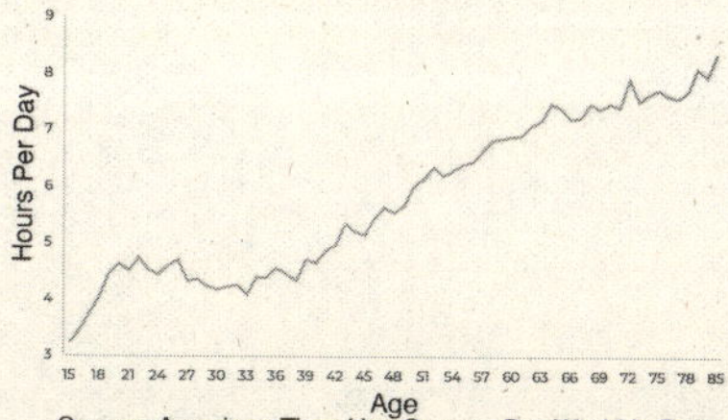

Source: American Time Use Survey, Our World in Data

Data shows that the time we spend with children peaks in our 30s and declines over the course of our life. On the other hand, time spent alone steadily increases throughout life.

Being present and savouring the sweet moments have never been more essential. Nurturing bonds with our children in the few years that we spend most of the time with them involves non-attachment and a breaking away of the tightly knit circles of me, mine and my ideas. The earlier in life that we identify and embrace our core values, the easier it will be when we have to deal with solitude and learn to flex the boredom muscle regularly.

Most importantly, practising compassion with our family, and later on, practising self-compassion when we are alone is not only a tool for happiness, but also for survival.

Swim the seas, watch the dolphins and embrace the high tides as you get mindfulness right by minding all four aspects of mindfulness.

15

Mindfulness Champions

Success Stories on Mindful Living

For over two hundred pages, you have heard from us, from researchers and clients about mindfulness, the practice and the everlasting impact it has on lives.

Now, we introduce real-life champions of mindfulness who are also eminent figures who practise mindfulness as a way of life. Like us, they have had their share of difficulties, stressful situations and strifes with loved ones. But mindfulness has come to their rescue in more ways than one. This chapter is based on direct interviews with Dr Kiran Bedi, India's first woman IPS officer; National Award–winning director Shonali Bose; ex-CEA K.V. Subramanian; happiness researcher and author Dr Raj Raghunathan; and Bajaj Allianz General Insurance CEO and MD Tapan Singhel.

If you are still unsure about how mindfulness can help, we hope this chapter will erase any further doubts and inspire you to practise mindfulness diligently.

SHONALI BOSE: 'Self-compassion and self-love help you deal with shame and guilt'[1]

For most people, the sky is blue or pink depending on the time of day. But for Shonali Bose, it seemed like the sky was iridescent at all times. Born in Kolkata, Shonali was a student of history and political science, practitioner of yoga and excited about all things healthy. Seeing films as the means to communicate ideas about social and political change, she started creating magic onscreen to showcase issues off-screen. Her debut film, *Amu*, won her the National Film Award for Best Feature Film in English. Her stature as a filmmaker grew following the critical and commercial success of *Margarita with a Straw*, *The Sky Is Pink* and *Raat Rani*. But not all was rosy in this talented and driven lady's life. At the age of twenty-one, she lost her mother due to medical negligence. She chose to suppress the pain and grief for years until, twenty-five years later, the centre of her universe was shattered once again. Her firstborn, Ishan, succumbed in a fire accident right before her eyes. This time, however, she chose to sit with the pain. However unbearable it was.

***

Shonali's house in Los Angeles though vast in size was empty. Her husband was in India and her second son, Vivan, was in school. She sat alone on the floor in the middle of her living room, on a red Kashmiri carpet, gazing at a framed picture of her late son Ishan, which she had carefully leaned against the fireplace. Shonali simply could not believe her life was engulfed

[1] In conversation with Swati, June 2022.

in heart-wrenching grief again. This time, she knew she had to do something different. Something different to stay afloat.

So, every day, for the next months, she dedicated time for grieving. For nine months, she sat alone with the darkest thoughts looming around her: *Why couldn't I save him*? And replaying what Ishan's father had told her, 'If I was there, I would have put the fire out.'

'These were like big black sentences in front of my eyes. It's a horrible thought. It's a thought you don't want in your brain. You just want to do something to banish the thought,' Shonali uttered as she recollected her period of grief. But she did not want to banish the thought. It was very difficult, but she just sat with it. Some days she was a puddle on the floor. But after some time the sobs would abate and she would get up calmly and be able to pick her younger child from school chattering cheerfully. She observed all the thoughts and feelings without diverting from them. Concentrating fiercely on the big black ugly sentences.

Being a disciplined yoga practitioner, Shonali decided to do yoga in front of Ishan's picture. Before his death, yoga was something she did with ease. However, in the beginning she found it almost impossible to resume the practice. She recollected that it was probably the focus on the sound of her breath which viscerally brought back the sound of the machine in the hospital room.

One day, she was doing a headstand and her leg slipped and broke the glass frame on Ishan's photo. That was when she wept and wept through the day, trying to forgive herself for not being able to save her son. Sitting with the thought of being unable to put the fire out, Shonali bravely re-enacted that fateful day, moment by moment and timed it. She stood in front of Ishan's bathroom mirror where he had been shaving. Then ran out to the kitchen (this is when she heard him screaming and came running down from her own bedroom) where he tried to pull open the back door while she and her younger son kept trying to beat out the flames. And then followed him as he ran back through the kitchen, out of the front door, down the driveway of the house, across the garden at the back, through the little gate and into the swimming pool. Brilliant. Ishan knew what to do in the middle of his own terror and pain. And this fact really killed her. Until she realised in doing the experiment that this entire sequence etched in her memory as lasting for minutes and feeling like hours was only all of 36 seconds!

Dwelling with the dark thoughts and re-enacting helped her realise that 36 seconds were too short for a sane human to act, let alone a mother seeing her son engulfed in flames. What followed was self-compassion and she was finally able to forgive herself.

During her grieving period, Shonali joined my weekly mindfulness practice group in Los Angeles. My daughter knew Ishan; they studied in the same school. Shonali found it very healing to do this course. At the end of nine months, she also attended her first mindfulness residential retreat in Spirit Rock in Northern California. It was a silent retreat and you could not use any device or even read a book. She had never meditated in her life and this was a ten-day vipassana course. Shonali's family in India was very worried as they spoke to her daily. She told them, 'What's the worst that will happen? I'll weep every day.'

However, the opposite happened. During a meditation session in a hall of over fifty people all of whom were crying silently at one point or the other, she found herself feeling euphoric and joyous. She started to see Ishan amidst the Nature on her walks, she saw him in every person meditating and felt a deep connection. On the last day, everyone breaks their silence and speaks about their experience. Shonali spoke about how she was conscious of her body for the first time in her life when she was pregnant with Ishan. She thought about what she ate and thought about the foetus growing within her for nine months. Coincidentally, it was exactly for nine months that she consciously cradled her feelings around the death of that same baby—sixteen years later.

Her meditation teacher remarked, 'In Buddhism, we say, you transcend pain if you embrace it.'

And that is what had happened with Shonali. She fiercely embraced her pain. She called it 'grief work' and sat with it daily in front of Ishan's photograph in her living room. She did not distract herself from the feelings and thoughts even with positive things like meditation. And in doing this daily exercise she transcended her pain and found deep peace and acceptance. The teacher explained the second thing that happened to Shonali as 'insight'. This usually happens after years of rigorous meditation but can sometimes happen through pain. In her extreme grief, Shonali had gained perspective about life and death and felt completely connected with Ishan's spirit. The epiphany came to her when she was sitting on her bed and gazing at his smiling face in the framed photo. She heard his voice clear as day—'Mamma, I didn't need to be on earth any more'.

She also felt light and energy enter her body and vibrate intensely making her feel euphoric. An extreme joy akin to what moksha must be. It was not a new experience. Twenty-five years prior when she was putting her mother's ashes in the ocean—she saw her mother and felt the same light and energy enter her. She felt superhumanly strong for three days. But after that she let it go. She did not believe it was real and turned her back on spirituality.

Now when Ishan spoke and she experienced the same energy and light, she knew this was for real. And she also immediately understood the meaning of his words. In Hindusim, it is believed that a soul takes shape in a body on earth to go through a journey and learn certain lessons that that soul needs to learn in this life. When those lessons are learned, the soul does not need to remain in the body any longer. Only very advanced souls die young.

It was life-changing for Shonali to know that she was blessed with two souls who were meant to be on earth only for a short period of time—her mother and her son. Thereafter, she chose to celebrate death as much as she chose to celebrate life.

The mindfulness course gave her 'structure and language to deal with life by sitting with what was uncomfortable and difficult'. It made her welcome pain as her biggest teacher. She took every bad thing that happened to her as an opportunity to learn. To experience self-growth.

'The practice of self-love which is considered narcissistic by many is one of the most important things to learn in life.'

'One of the other things I loved about your course, Swati, is where we meditate, keeping the most difficult person in one's life in our thoughts and give them compassion, that was life-changing,' Shonali recollected. 'But harder than the difficult person is focusing on oneself and giving oneself compassion. We are harsh and unforgiving with ourselves, with things we have done in the past, with how we judge our bodies. The practice of self-love which is considered narcissistic by many is one of the most important things to learn in life.

Self-compassion and self-love help you deal with shame and guilt. Because if you are not able to forgive yourself, you will not be able to live freely or have healthy relationships with others.' Shonali cited this as one of her biggest learnings in life.

All of this sounds easier said than done. But it comes with practice. After practising mindfulness for years, Shonali became a deep advocate of self-compassion. She believed in a simple principle to overcome guilt: 'You have to release yourself (with self-compassion) and know you can't control how "others" behave towards you; you can only control how you react to their behaviour.'

Compassion for the most difficult person at that moment, self-compassion and sitting with pain were the three factors that proved life-changing for her.

***

Shonali did not limit compassion to herself and her family. In every work of hers, from *Amu* and *Margarita with a Straw* to *The Sky Is Pink* and recently, *Raat Rani*, Shonali formed a deep connection with each of her actors. She felt like a mother to them, not because of her age and experience but because she made sure she had their back.

At the end of the shooting of the film *The Sky Is Pink*, the actors Priyanka Chopra, Farhan Akhtar, Zaira Wasim and Rohit Saraf told Shonali, 'We feel healed by you. Not only by the subject of the film but by working with you.'

That was the impact of compassion and emotional energy Shonali invested which brought out the best performance in each actor.

After every shot, when shouting cut, Shonali would walk up to the actor and offer a hug to celebrate their shot. In one scene in *The Sky Is Pink*, Priyanka broke down while watching a video of her dead daughter. Shonali shouted cut and walked up to Priyanka and hugged her. But Priyanka did not let go and clung on to Shonali, gasping for breath like she was wheezing and uttered, 'I am sorry for Ishlu … I am so sorry for Ishlu …'

While doing the film, Priyanka internalised Shonali's pain and performed as if she was her. The mother who had lost her son. That was the connection that had been formed between the director and the actor.

Zaira Wasim was suffering from depression and had quit acting before she signed *The Sky Is Pink*. Shonali was the reason for her change of mind. Shonali flew to Kashmir to be with her and talk to her. Shonali did an exercise with Zaira for two days: played a lot of music and danced till her heart and whole body burned out. Followed by lying still in shavasana position while Shonali gently guided light to enter her body. In two days, Zaira's mother saw a changed person who went on to do Shonali's film before quitting acting finally. There was no coercion or monetary motives involved in getting Zaira to sign up for the movie. Only compassion and an emotional connect.

'I form an umbilical cord between me and the actor. An actor is so vulnerable. They are emotionally naked when on set.'

Shonali herself remained vulnerable as a director. If another person was emotionally naked, she felt it was important to be emotionally naked with them too. While directing *Margarita with a Straw* there was a scene when the mother was dying in hospital—almost exactly as her own mother died. A silent wail erupted from her body while the shot was on. But Shonali was not embarrassed about going to pieces so publicly in front of a hundred-odd crew, mostly men. Later, she took the time to speak with every person about what was going on with her. The movie was shot soon after Ishan's death, so her feelings were raw. The extraordinary ability to be so vulnerable while in a commanding position where everyone expects you to be as tough as nails has created the sensitive emotional cinema Shonali is known for. She said that remaining open and in tune with her feelings opened up her creativity instead of suppressing it.

Whether on set or off, Shonali lived her life with ease and joy and was an authentic person in the artificial tinsel world of Bollywood. She was that rare person who used something as frivolous as social media to talk honestly and rawly about death. Her motto in life was to always see the glass as half full and be supremely grateful and optimistic. 'Life is only a journey—don't take it so seriously and death is just another address. A party in the Pink Sky that we are all headed to. How happy is that thought!'

KIRAN BEDI: 'If you are joyful within, how will you make others sad?'[2]

In a large hall of hundreds of male police officers, sat one female officer, cross-legged and eyes closed, leading from the front—Dr Kiran Bedi. The officers convened not to prepare for a security threat but for a rigorous training of a different kind. A training of the mind, auditing internally and nourishing the body and soul with 'psychological food'.

Dr Kiran Bedi is known to be the first woman to have joined the ranks of Indian Police Service, an author of several books, fearless leader who stands for the last man and a recipient of the Ramon Magsaysay award for prison reforms.

No wonder, she is a household name.

However, we want you to see her as a mindfulness champion and a beacon of equanimity, compassion and non-attachment through her practice of vipassana and mindfulness.

In 1993, Dr Bedi was posted as inspector general to Tihar Jail, notorious for inhumane conditions, violence, drug use and gang fights. Tihar housed close to ten thousand prisoners

[2] In conversation with authors, July 2022.

and with Dr Bedi in charge, a sea of change was to follow. She wanted to treat the prisoners for who they rightly were—humans.

As narrated in the documentary *Doing Time, Doing Vipassana*: 'India is a land of paradox, where else will you find a prisoner crying like a child in the arms of a jailer?' And that change in Tihar started with Dr Bedi's intent and a suggestion by the young officer Rajinder Kumar, who knew of 'a magical therapy to get the inmates rid themselves of corrosive emotions'.

This is how Dr Bedi recollected learning about vipassana for the first time. 'Vipassana is a Pali word which means looking at yourself in a special way. Prisoners were suffering from anger, revenge and hatefulness; all negative feelings. And I was looking for a solution.'

Convinced that vipassana made Rajinder an improved man whose violent eruptions at home had stopped with meditations, she boldly introduced it in prison.

But she started with the change agents first, the police officers. With the help of Ram Singh, a vipassana teacher and former home secretary of Rajasthan, a ten-day vipassana retreat in Jaipur converted even the toughest of the officers. Even the most aggressive police officers who believed in punishment became calmer and less reactive.

Ram Singh chose a handful of prisoners to participate in the course. Dr Bedi recollected that these were the most difficult offenders; the ones convicted of heinous acts of crime and had nothing to look forward to in life.

> ***'Crime and delinquency are a thought–action product. It is intertwined. In order to correct action, we cannot ignore the thought process.'***
>
> **—Kiran Bedi,**
> ***It's Always Possible***

The prisoners threatened to hit and bite the officers and teachers but the teachers responded with equal gumption, 'Okay! Hit us! We are not afraid of you and we will not hit you back.' And that is where love and kindness slowly took over the culture of punishment in Tihar Jail.

For the first three days, meditation made participants focus on breathing patterns (explained earlier in this book). The remaining seven days were devoted to becoming conscious of body sensations and emotions and how to control them.

On the eighth day a prisoner said, 'My mind kept wandering first and then I became aware of physical sensations. And slowly realised it is my reaction to pleasant and unpleasant sensations that leads to crime. It is you who can go on the right path—answer lies within you.'

On the final day of the session, Dr Bedi said, 'When the prisoners were acting instead of reacting, that is when it all changed and the prisoners broke down asking for forgiveness.'

Even a prisoner convicted of triple murder pleaded for forgiveness, vowing to never commit crime again.

The results were phenomenal:

Bichittar Singh, a prisoner serving a life term was plotting revenge against his parents until the ten-day course.

Santokh Singh who was charged with murder expressed that the meditation had brought him peace of mind.

Sattbir Singh, an ex-constable serving ten years for rape for no fault of his, confessed, 'I used to think the stick was all powerful but now I think love and affection have greater powers!'

***

Curious to know Dr Bedi's personal experience with mindfulness, we asked her how vipassana helped her deal with difficulties in her career, personal life and politics.

'My whole life changed after that. My reactions were more balanced, more real. I became action-oriented and not reaction-oriented!' She exclaimed happily.

Dr Bedi first did the vipassana meditation at the Police Training Centre in Delhi.

'It was more difficult to coax officers as they thought nothing was wrong with them. In fact, they were worse off than prisoners,' Dr Bedi told us. That is when she knew she had to lead the entire team of officers by example.

Rather than condemning offenders immediately, Dr Bedi started understanding reality and observing herself and approached the offenders with compassion and not out of spite or revenge.

Many believe fearlessness is genetic and granted only to a few. But Dr Bedi told us, 'When you become more realistic in life, you become fearless.'

She viewed life as developments and not as fears to be conquered. Life comes with all challenges; grief is part of life as much as joy. And this fearlessness and sense of freedom arose in her from practising the techniques learnt through vipassana. For Dr Bedi, the first course was like a seed sown and as she went through life, the plant kept growing.

Non-attachment, according to Dr Bedi, not only meant accepting the Law of Impermanence, but also not expecting the external world to always support you. Knowing that one has no control over life's outcomes such as death makes you realise that some things belong to you but not forever.

Accepting that everything, even the moment you are blinking now, is impermanent helped Dr Bedi cope with the loss of her parents, sister and brother-in-law. She started focusing on the years spent together with them and not the years lost. She felt a sense of gratitude for the seventy years she spent with her parents. The grief and the pain were felt but not prolonged.

When we asked Dr Bedi how she managed personal relationships especially when people pushed her buttons, she replied, 'by raising my tolerance and accepting their limitations'.

Dr Bedi said it is easier said than done but to maintain relationships, it is also important to reduce expectations of them.

With age, experience, meditation practice and time, one learns to shorten the pain and conflicts by observing, 'Sharper your observation, shorter the duration of disturbance and reactivity. If you are at peace with yourself, how will you make others angry?'

'Compassion and love have just grown and grown over the years,' Dr Bedi said. It completely changed her outlook on life and has kept her happy and settled. For Dr Bedi, vipassana is beyond mindfulness. She called it 'fullness'. Instead of revenge and spite, Dr Bedi does not see what the other person (politician or prisoner) did wrong but asks, 'What can I do for them?' And that is when she chooses to respond with love and compassion without judgement and without expecting them to reciprocate in the same way.

However, this does not mean there was no conflict or clash against Dr Bedi's core values. As an anti-corruption crusader and proponent of proper law enforcement, Dr Bedi ensured that the law was always enforced. She is known to have got even Prime Minister Indira Gandhi's car towed for illegal parking.

What particularly interested us in our conversation with Dr Bedi was when she said she does not use hurtful or aggressive language. Instead of '*dekh lenge*', she responds to the haters with '*kar lenge*'. As Dr Bedi affirmed, 'If you are joyful within, how will you make others sad?' Breaking of ego gives way to larger giving.

***

In the documentary *Kiran Bedi*: *Yes Madam, Sir*, Dr Bedi's daughter says, 'Marriage is a lot of giving. Marriage is a full-time commitment. My mother is married to her work.'

It is undeniable that passion fuelled Dr Bedi's success in an incredibly challenging profession such as the police forces and politics. One of the most common misconceptions about mindfulness is that it will kill passion and subdue energy. When we discussed this with Dr Bedi, she fervently shook her head in disagreement. She strongly believed that practising mindfulness gave her more energy to pursue her passion, but it is purer in form. It motivated her to want to do better and focus on collaboration instead of competition.

There is a shift from selfishness to empowerment of others when you practise non-attachment and compassion. In *Yes Madam, Sir*, Dr Bedi admits, 'I have lived a very prioritised and focused life. Work has always been my priority. My family got how much I thought they needed.'

'When you practice passion with mindfulness, you stop biting. You just start chewing. It is not that you are not eating. You don't lose your hunger but you chew more. And you don't bite. You don't steal. You don't snatch. You savour the passion more.'

Passion therefore complements the mindfulness practice, helping one to stay true to the law of Nature. And that is dharma. Her analogy of comparing pursuit of passion with nourishment and biting blew our minds and we are sure it will sit well with you as well.

***

Today's youth have a plethora of opportunities to choose from but are also living in a world divided by hate. Dr Bedi advised them to accept responsibility.

'You have a choice to accept responsibility. Once accepted, you belong to it. Then come what may, take it one day at a time. Respond, don't react. Grow in it, deal with it and do your own duty, no matter what.'

Dr Bedi draws us in with her inspiring life, warm smile and clear-headed attitude towards life. One can learn from her past and present and know that nothing in life is permanent.

There is a thin line between prisoners and jailers and in fact, in our minds, we are all potential criminals. So, we would like to end with this anecdote.

One prisoner who learnt to forgive himself through vipassana timidly asked Dr Bedi, 'Madam, how many people in the world believe they are here to just do good? What percentage?'

Dr Bedi smiles, looks at him and all the prisoners, saying, 'You are that percentage!'

RAJ RAGHUNATHAN: 'Do small things with great love'[3]

On a large stage with flashing lights and a bright red TED sign on it, stood King Khan announcing, 'Why are some people still unhappy despite having it all in life? And some people are happy despite having very little? To answer these questions, we have the scholar and professor of happiness Dr Raj Raghunathan!'

Only a handful in this world get to be introduced by superstar Shah Rukh Khan to an audience with great applause and the moniker, professor of happiness.

---

[3] In conversation with authors, September 2022.

Dr Raj was one of them. As he got on stage with a bright smile and a skip in his step, no one would know he had waited twelve hours cooped up in a room, fighting severe jet lag. But before you try to satiate your curiosity by skipping ahead and reading about Dr Raj's onstage banter with King Khan, we would like you to read about how a happiness expert employed mindfulness and his own journey with vipassana.

Dr Raj, a happiness expert and bestselling author, credited mindfulness as a reliable source of increasing happiness. However, in practice, he felt like an amateur. Hence, Dr Raj chose to immerse himself in a vipassana course at a retreat.

As the meditations started, Dr Raj was determined to take the experience seriously like an ardent student. He woke up at 4:30 a.m. every day, practised silence and even attempted difficult and painful meditations like the *adhishatha* in which the meditator sits like a still statue for one hour.

Dr Raj's experience with vipassana was revelatory and shocking. Before the retreat, he had been suffering from sciatica for many years. The pain was so unbearable that he would have to lift himself up with both hands when he got out of bed every morning.

During the course, the pain started to flare up again but Dr Raj embraced it in his determination to be an obedient student. 'We were asked to observe the pain or pleasure without getting attached to either, without wanting more of the former and without wanting the latter to end.'

Every night, after a whole day of strenuous and painful meditations, the pain would return. And that too with a vengeance. What would start as cramps in his feet would start to move up his legs to his back. Dr Raj resisted the sensations at first, he would walk or stand on his toes to subside the cramps. Alone in his room, with no one to talk to, Dr Raj lost sleep for three nights because his body would involuntarily make movements throughout the night.

Completely confused about how his body was reacting, he tried to talk to the coordinators. Unfortunately, the coordinators were all Vietnamese and none of them could understand Dr Raj and vice versa. So, Dr Raj adopted the next best option at hand, he let go of all control of his body and let it take its course at night.

The cramps began at the sole of his feet, bending his toes into a clawed position and feet turning inwards. In sudden jerks, one of his legs shot up in the air in 90 degrees and his arms shot up the same way. Dr Raj recollected that to an outsider, it would have seemed like yoga poses or a person possessed.

The cramps and jerk-like movements did not stop. It crept up his spine, to his neck and to the top of his head and forced him into a bridge pose. As Dr Raj's head touched the floor, his back pushing hips towards the ceiling, he heard a series of cracks and sounds that straightened his back.

Miraculously, his back was now like a teenager's! Ironically, letting go of the control over his body and mind allowed Dr Raj to gain control of his body again. He was able to bend forward and backward after suffering for eight years. And all this happened completely involuntarily!

Later, when Dr Raj spoke to a neurologist about his experience, the revelations he learnt were refreshing. 'Our body is always trying to fix itself and that's probably what my body was doing, trying to fix itself through cramps,' narrated Dr Raj.

'Mindfulness practice teaches you non-attachment. It gives you the ability to separate your mind from where it wants to go versus where it should go.'

The next day, during meditation, his neck started moving involuntarily as well, shaking side to side and trying to rotate nearly 360 degrees like the famous scene from *Omen*. This time, Dr Raj stopped his body in fear of being possessed. In hindsight, he believed it could have been his body trying to fix his upper back and neck issues.

***

It is important to talk about depression. Globally, an estimated 5 per cent of adults (or approximately 280 million people) suffer from it (WHO website, 13 March 2023). The mental illness can be of many types—clinical, induced by chemical imbalances, trauma-related or even periodical. Dr Raj was honest and open about his experience with depression and how some of the episodes that flashed through his mind felt like it was the end of the world.

'Wanting to be happy is one thing but unless you put in place a bunch of action items, it is not going to happen,' Dr Raj observed. The stigma around depression needs to be broken. And should be viewed as a project like weight loss or career change instead of just 'stop being weak'.

It is only when Dr Raj faced depression himself that he got interested in the topic of happiness and decided that 'the best way to learn about a topic is to teach it.' In the process of learning and researching about happiness, he was able to *a*. zero in on things that have the highest impact on happiness, *b*. prioritise them and *c*. implement them in order of priority.

Mindfulness, especially non-attachment, emerged as one of the key drivers of happiness. With the help of mindfulness practice, Dr Raj started observing casual changes in himself; how overconsumption of alcohol made him feel low and how little control he had over his emotions. A sense of self-awareness emerged with the mindfulness practice.

Dr Raj contributed improvement in happiness to two things. First, a healthy lifestyle, which includes eating well, having a good sleep routine and exercising for minimum thirty minutes a day. Second, maintaining a healthy and positive attitude.

Happiness gravitates more towards those who practise gratitude and are kind and compassionate, and pursue passion with non-attachment.

Dr Raj interviewed Dr Richard Davidson, the neuropsychologist who researched brains of Buddhist monks to see the structural differences with non-meditators, for the Happiness course on Coursera. Dr Davidson observed that it is enough to practise meditation and mindfulness for only two minutes daily because regularity is more important than the duration.

Dr Raj followed this advice religiously. Every night, he sat to meditate for at least two minutes. The meditation he chose to do is a version of the body scan where he starts with observing his breath, body sensations and feelings/thoughts. He ends his meditation with the following affirmations, 'Life is good because I always can come back to this present moment.'

Over the last eight years, Dr Raj has only missed ten days of not practising mindfulness meditations. He affirmed that mindfulness meditations 'teaches you non-attachment. Every moment you bring your mind back to the present, you train it to separate from what the mind is attracted to and bring it back to reality.' In other words, this practice allows you to guide your mind from where it wants to go as opposed to where it should go.

In effect, mindfulness 'makes it easier for you to prioritise things in life'. It helps you to focus on a presentation instead of watching a cricket match. It helps you to put your phone down when having dinner with your friend. In an argument, it helps you from saying the next angry thing and not reacting.

Being compassionate is a huge component of being happy. While research and studies show this, Dr Raj was surprised when he discovered this. Dr Raj is a professor of marketing at the business school in the University of Austin, Texas.

Teaching in a business school made Dr Raj view compassion as large-scale donations or things that create maximum value or utility for many people, in other words philanthropy. He was sceptical about how small acts of love and kindness contribute to happiness but he was pleasantly surprised.

'Do small things with great love.' Dr Raj observed that this was the best way to approach kindness. Smile at a stranger. Buy a small or surprise gift for someone special. In a meeting, allow others to talk even if you have the same ideas. Sometimes, kindness can be offered in places you least expect it; even in a bar. At times, Dr Raj, after a night of binge drinking, would not only buy himself a bottle of water to hydrate but also end up buying water for everyone present there as an act of kindness.

Ironically, it is also hardest to show compassion to those who are dearest to you—the ones with shared goals such as your spouse. Because when one cares, the arguments and conflicts are heated with ego getting in the way.

To address this with compassion, Dr Raj added a loving kindness component to his affirmations. At bedtime daily, he whispered wishes to both his loved ones and enemies: 'May they be peaceful. May they be loved.'

Sending good vibes and love to those who are close, even when he does not feel like it, allowed Dr Raj to smile and show more empathy and less reactivity in arguments.

***

And cut! To those of you who are curious, how does being a speaker on TED India show, hosted by Shah Rukh Khan have anything to do with mindfulness? And how can two minutes of fame be a lesson in non-attachment?

23 August 2017.

Dr Raj remembered the day like it was yesterday—his first TED talk, hosted by Shah Rukh Khan at Yash Raj studio, standing amidst posters of legendary movies like *Dilwale Dulhania Le Jayenge* and *Sholay*. Dr Raj was trying to take it all in and pinching himself in excitement. He was instructed to come to the sets at 11 a.m. so that shooting could commence at 3:30 p.m.

Although it is not his native language, Dr Raj had worked hard to compress a complicated topic such as happiness into a five-minute speech in Hindi. Not just that, he was battling jet lag after his journey from Austin to Mumbai.

Valuing punctuality, Dr Raj arrived at 11 a.m. and was cooped up in his room with occasional visits from the make-up artists and organisers. At 3:30 p.m., there was no sign of either King Khan or the show commencing. And no news until almost 8 p.m.! Alone in his room, cooped up with only his speech notes and some food, Dr Raj was getting restless and borderline angry.

The audience waiting since 11 a.m. was being entertained but Dr Raj felt jittery, twiddling his thumbs in a room all alone. Also, he had the permission to interview Shah Rukh Khan about employee well-being for his Coursera course and thought he would never get a chance to do so!

That is when his mind started wandering: *Who does Shah Rukh think he is? How can he show up so late and not respect anyone else's time?*

Dr Raj knew these thoughts needed to be stopped before they became a vicious cycle of negativity.

So, he stood up, stretched and sat on a chair outside his room and started meditating. He started focusing on his body and his breath, bringing his mind to the present. His thoughts slowly started changing. *I started disassociating from feelings of anger and resentment. Shah Rukh is such a busy personality; I don't know what his schedule is and it is okay if I am waiting as long as my speech goes well.*

That is when he heard commotion all around him. King Khan was walking past with his entourage! And when Dr Raj opened his eyes, Shah Rukh smiled at him (a very endearing, dimpled smile) and Dr Raj smiled back, his mood uplifting instantly.

The five-minute TED talk went very well as planned and Shah Rukh came to have a light, on-stage banter with Dr Raj.

'*Tum kitne khush ho*?'

Dr Raj answered, 'On a scale of 1–10, I am a 9.23!'

'And how did you pick 9.23?'

'Until I met you, I was 9.22 but after I met you, I am 9.23!'

'Oh! So, it is not your practice that makes you happy but *me* that makes you 9.23 happy!'

The crowd burst into laughter and so did Dr Raj.

But what followed next was the real icing on the cake.

Shah Rukh said, 'I saw him backstage, preparing for his speech. I have seen a lot of people prepare their speech; somebody is sweating, somebody is pacing up and down. But he was so relaxed, meditating with eyes closed. But his meditative quality is working on him. And according to me, he is not 9.23 but a 10/10!'

If this story does not motivate you to practise mindfulness, breathe deep and do a body scan, you may think otherwise.

KRISHNAMURTHY V. SUBRAMANIAN: 'If morals and values are not adopted, spiritual progress will be very slow'[4]

Serving as the chief economic advisor (CEA) to the Government of India is no small feat, let alone serving during the thickness of a once-in-a-century pandemic. From 2018 to 2021, Dr Subramanian served as CEA with immense scrutiny from the media and the public on how a pandemic would be managed.

A top-ranking Indian Institute of Technology (IIT) Kanpur alumnus, an MBA from the Indian Institute of Management (IIM) Calcutta, a PhD from the University of Chicago, a professor at the Indian School of Business (ISB) and currently the executive director at the International Monetary Fund (IMF), Dr Subramanian attributed his success to hard work, merit and most importantly, his father.

Unlike the CEAs that preceded him, Dr Subramanian hails from a family that was not rich in power, wealth or pedagogy but immensely rich in the ambition they had and the courage with which they imbibed values in both Dr Subramanian and his brother.

'Spirituality enables you to live life king-size. It is not about how big your car is or how large your house is. It is about the equanimity with which you react to people, situations and events.'

Dr Subramanian asserted that without his father, he would be nothing. Working hard and doing what is right instead of doing what is popular is a core value Dr Subramanian has lived with. In other words, the courage to live your own story even when adverse circumstances may cry out loud for you to follow the herd.

---

[4] In conversation with authors, November 2022.

As we have discussed, core values and compassion help resolve conflicts and enable clearer decision-making. Without them, non-attachment and present-moment awareness are suboptimal.

Dr Subramanian agreed. 'Many people work hard but the universe supports you if you have pure thoughts and intentions. If morals and values are not adopted, spiritual progress will be very slow.'

Watching his parents struggle, Dr Subramanian reiterated that it was the values he saw his father exemplify that led to a life of success and rewards. He was the first one in the family to step into the hallowed portals of IIT. And soon, Dr Subramanian's father became famous in their social circle as being the father of two top-ranking sons at the IIT.

While most of the world knows Dr Subramanian's story as an astute economic advisor, we knew him from his days as an academic at the Indian School of Business.

***

'*Itni hi kahani teri?* (Is your story only this much?)'

Dr Subramanian was asked by his brother—younger by two years—during their days in IIT Kanpur. On a wintery evening in his hostel room, his brother started probing his life's purpose with the question, '*Agle saal tera job lag jayega, uske baad tu kya karega*? (You will get a job next year, what will you do next?) '

One after the other, Dr Subramanian visualised different stages in his life unfolding as his brother kept probing, '*Uske baad kya karega*? (What next?)' He ended up narrating to his brother how events in his life will unfold from a job through marriage and kids to eventual death. Almost like it was that simple. That is when his brother forced him to answer the ultimate question every human must ask, '*What is the purpose of my life?*'

His brother also introduced him to the term, *vivek* or discrimination. Vivek is what differentiates humans from animals. An animal that has eaten and is full, will not eat a prey even if it is around. Whereas, humans may be full but still overeat if something tempting is offered to them. Likewise, even in extreme hunger, a human will not eat something unpalatable. On the other hand, an animal will listen only to hunger pangs and eat what is available

Dr Subramanian believes that this understanding of *vivek* or discrimination is where the essence of spiritual progress lies.

Dr Subramanian began his mindfulness journey in earnest while pursuing his PhD at the University of Chicago. Just a few weeks after moving from India to pursue his PhD, his friend sent him an email raving about the Art of Living (AOL) course he had done recently. Dr Subramanian regretted not having undertaken the course when he was in India and being stuck in an alien country so far from the spiritual cradle of the world, India.

'Never delay a good thing!' he told himself, immediately registering for the course and planting the first seed of spirituality in his life.

He listened to the claim Sri Sri Ravi Shankar made that *attention can melt away pain*.

But this belief was not consistent with his own experience of the meditations. The tree for spirituality therefore grew with his experience with vipassana.

In 2005, Dr Subramanian attended his first vipassana retreat. Motivated by the videos he watched of Goenkaji, he was determined to not waste any moment and give it his all at the course.

For him listening and believing in Goenkaji's lectures had to begin with open-mindedness. He hailed from an orthodox Brahmin family that diligently adhered to all Hindu rituals, an aspect that Goenkaji abhorred. Goenkaji believed in pure path of rationality. As he sat for the *anapana* meditation, focusing on the breath at the tip of his nose, Dr Subramanian could make the connection with the Bhagavad Gita.

In the Gita, Lord Krishna advices Prince Arjuna to sit still by focusing the breath and gaze on the tip of his nose—a technique so ancient yet applicable in modern times that can lead to focusing on the present moment.

On the eighth day of the ten-day long vipassana retreat, as Dr Subramanian sat still like a statue in *Adhishthan Bhaithak*, he suffered extreme pain. He could sit still for 40–45 minutes but the pain in his legs and body became increasingly excruciating. He had tried sitting still like a rock without any movement on the sixth and seventh days and gave up after possibly 40–45 minutes.

'The pain will not kill me. Even if it kills me, I will at least die while meditating,' he told himself on the eighth day, determined to stay still and as was the instruction from Goenkaji, focusing all his attention on the precise area in his legs where he experienced the pain. At about the 50th minute, something miraculous happened, the pain simply melted away!

And that was when he was truly able to experience what Sri Sri advised, attention that is not prejudiced (or *sakshi bhav*) can be enlightening! Along with this realisation, came an important advice to us all. Dr Subramanian encouraged everyone to experience the mindfulness journey for themselves without judgement.

He did the vipassana course four times but all his revelations came to him only in the first experience. In the consequent sessions, he sat down, expecting epiphany but it never came, leading to another realisation:

'Path dependence is a financial term and that's what I learnt—but in spirituality, you should practise with no path dependence and no expectations!'

'I am a big fan of logic because it is a superset of science,' Dr Subramanian told us and was in awe of the logical distillation of Buddha's explanation of life. He learnt the essence of life, as defined by Buddha, in only two principles.

First, all of life's actions are driven by only two things—craving for pleasurable experiences and aversion to unpleasurable experiences.

Second, all cravings and aversions eventually manifest as physical experiences in the '*Dhai hath ki kaya* (in this fathom long body)'. It is this understanding of craving and aversion that allowed him to balance the decisions made by the heart versus the mind. This understanding also grounded him and made him open to experiences that he did not observe in his scholars and peers who were stuck in their own ways of doing things. Along with this balance of craving and aversions, came a true understanding of non-attachment and impermanence.

In 2018, when Dr Subramanian became the CEA, he rose to celebrity status and was adulated and scrutinised by the public and the media. Suddenly, from being a professor surrounded by students, he became an icon constantly surrounded by media men!

'I enjoyed the adulation but never hankered for it,' Dr Subramanian said. 'Every time the camera clicked, I used to think, *sab anitya hain* (everything is impermanent). *This will also pass, so enjoy it while it lasts.*

Keeping unprejudiced awareness allowed him to enjoy the post, and non-attachment allowed him to resist any craving for fame and continue to do what is right for the nation.

During his PhD days in Chicago, Dr Subramanian observed that most Americans and elite Indians attribute success to their ability and failure to external factors. One trained in non-attachment realises the opposite—success is as much an outcome of luck as it is of ability. Worshipping success and not recognising the huge contribution of luck is what induces the craving for more success and fame.

In March 2020, Dr Subramanian was tasked with advising the Indian economy amidst a once-in-a-century pandemic. A pandemic with its multiple waves sent shocks not only to the economy, but also to many lives and livelihoods. Ever since doing the vipassana courses, Dr Subramanian had vivid dreams which felt like an extension of his reality.

One such dream occurred the day before Dr Subramanian was to present to Prime Minister Narendra Modi on key decisions the Indian economy needed to take during the pandemic. After working late on the presentation that night, Dr Subramanian went to sleep. In his sleep, his late father woke him up vehemently.

His father told Dr Subramanian that he needs to wake up early to study because he has missed something in his syllabus. In the dream, Dr Subramanian argued that he need not study any more as he was a professor! However, his father refused to listen and said one last time, 'You have unfinished business!'

Startled, Dr Subramanian woke up at 5 a.m. and immediately started to work on completing his presentation, realising that he may have covered all the points but had not thought about how to exposit it to the prime minister.

'It doesn't matter that 99.99999 per cent of people will not believe this. That dream helped me perfect a presentation that changed the course of India's history during the pandemic!' Dr Subramanian reflected.

While the US and other advanced economies were spending money as if there was no tomorrow, Dr Subramanian did not think it was the right strategy for India. Almost all economic commentators and politicians were urging him to spend more on the economy. Dr Subramanian did not relent.

The resilience to do what is right can be credited to his mindfulness practice. Against all odds, Dr Subramanian advised a lockdown. His team's research indicated that if a lockdown was not in place, there would be close to 100,000 deaths by May 2020.

'*Jaan rahega toh GDP wapas aa jayega, Sir*! (It is possible for GDP to return only if people are alive!)'

He told the PM as he wanted to protect India's most vulnerable—the poor.

He explained that in a poor household of five or six people, if the bread earner dies, the rest will be on the streets. Without a lockdown, such bread earners will not worry about the pandemic and imperil their lives. The lockdown led to a 25 per cent drop in GDP but with confidence, he told the media that as the CEA, he was playing the ball, not the bowler, and will be treating the pandemic as a 50-over match to strategise and win.

If he was worried only about his legacy, he would not have advised lockdown. His core values of integrity, belief in dharma and compassion towards the poor saved many lives and India's economy sustained through it all as it experienced a V-shaped recovery that he had predicted after the 25 per cent drop in GDP.

***

Another stressful task Dr Subramanian undertook as the CEA was to publish the economic survey report. As the CEA, he was the head of a cadre of over 700 Indian Economic Service officers. His own team working on the survey was about 60–70 officers and employees.

A month before the survey started, a senior member in his team joked, 'From now on, we will stay away from you because you will get stressed and we may get a piece of your mind.'

Dr Subramanian realised that prior experience had created this expectation among the senior staff members that the CEA would get stressed as the date for the presentation of the economic survey in Parliament nears and will lose his cool.

Dr Subramanian believed that a creative effort like writing the economic survey report cannot be delivered well by unhappy team members, so he decided to make a public commitment that he will not lose his cool and if he were to, he would pay the penalty by treating the entire team. The public commitment was Dr Subramanian's way of approaching his first economic survey with calculated calmness.

The commitment was also a way of imbibing a key characteristic of leadership that Dr Subramanian had observed in India's Captain Cool, Mahendra Singh Dhoni, who would remain calm even in the most stressful situations, thereby conveying that he was a leader in control. Dr Subramanian strongly believed that calmness helps to convey control.

Dr Subramanian knew from his spiritual experiences that only a calm mind can unleash creative potential. The research involved in generating the survey report is enormous and the writing and the presentation needs to be creative. As CEA, Dr Subramanian believed in leading by example. For 45–60 days before the survey was due, he practised meditation practices (*sadhana*) daily.

A week before the survey was due, at 9:30 at night, around fifty officials were all in his room in North Block, voicing their difficulties working on the survey because the Hindi translation was not happening. When he found the reasons for the Hindi translation not happening, internally, he was boiling but outwardly, Dr Subramanian kept his cool and said, 'I will find a way to take care of this.'

Without his mindfulness practice, Dr Subramanian believed he would not have been able to keep his calm nor would he have been able to complete the survey. No wonder, when he had the celebratory dinner after his first successful economic survey, his team called him their Captain Cool.

Dr Subramanian quoted the Greek story of Milo, the wrestler, to drive home his point on the mindfulness practice. From the time he was a boy, Milo would run carrying a calf every day. The calf kept growing into a bull leading to Milo eventually lifting a bull daily. His strength proved to be enormous helping him to win many athletic festivals. Sadhana is all about building this capacity. When faced with stress, our brain is no different and needs the capacity and strength to be resilient and different.

'If you sweat more during peacetime, you will bleed less during wartime. This applies to sadhana or spiritual practice as well.'

The biggest conundrum is this: the people who do not have time to do sadhana are the ones who need it the most. Dr Subramanian advocated that mindfulness practice needs to be your friend when you are in need. At the same time, when you are relaxed it is the best time to practise meditation because it prepares your brain for all that may come.

TAPAN SINGHEL: 'We are so polite to people we don't know, so why not with the ones we love?'[5]

In an office filled with photographs of a two-decade long journey as a leader at Bajaj Allianz General Insurance sat Tapan Singhel, MD and CEO, an aura of calm and composure surrounding him as he patiently explained to us that his journey in mindfulness had its roots in Buddha's teachings, the Bhagavad Gita and Patanjali Yoga Sutras.

Tapan is self-taught and applied the principles of mindfulness in everyday corporate life. His core value when it comes to Bajaj Allianz is: 'We do not build companies only for profit and quick hikes, we build companies for centuries!'

A scientist by qualification, Tapan had always been a curious man. When his journey started with Bajaj Allianz in 2001 in its first year of inception, he too joined the rat race with the burning desire to excel in his career.

'A lot of people think that when you become calmer, your ambitions drop. But with mindfulness, I am able to maximise my mental and physical strength and get a lot more done in the process.'

But somewhere down the line, he realised that the rat race was not the ultimatum. With the curiosity of a scientist, he started eagerly reading about meditation as followed by the Greeks, about dharma as discussed in the Bhagavad Gita and was inspired by Buddha's search for life's meaning. The seed to follow mindfulness in every aspect of life had been planted.

Being in the business of selling insurance, Tapan noticed that between the ages of forty-five and forty-eight is when the body

---

[5] In conversation with authors, November 2022.

starts ageing and a realisation dawns that one cannot function with the physical rigour of the twenties and a workout of the mental muscle is required to sustain dreams and ambitions.

'I used to be an alpha male, run 10 kilometres every day, smoke 30–40 cigarettes a day and lift 100 kgs of weight,' Tapan recollected. 'But after forty-five, I had to find a different way to maximise my mental and physical strength.'

The two tools that helped him transform his lifestyle were physical stretching through yoga and mental training through meditation and spirituality.

Life, according to Tapan, was divided into four parts of twenty-five years each and he believed that if you are physically aware of the changes happening in your body, you will be able to adopt mindfulness a lot earlier. For Tapan, mindfulness has translated into what he eats (*satvik* food) and making healthy choices (has quit smoking and drinking).It started with awareness of what the body needed and translated into a permanent change in lifestyle.

Tapan acknowledged that he achieved extreme clarity in thought through mindfulness. Instead of jumping to conclusions, decision-making at the executive level included finding solutions, powering innovation and resolving conflicts effectively among his employees. Importantly, compassion and empathy have become critical core values in the HR practice at Bajaj Allianz.

'Twenty or thirty years back, you were expected to be a cut-throat leader. In today's time, leaders need soft skills that include empathy and compassion.'

Compassion, according to him, enhanced his skills set to a different level. It started from the way he conducted meetings effectively to hiring and firing managers.

Compassion was in his smallest of actions. Tapan ensured his meetings were an efficient 15-minute discussion with little need for follow-up meetings. And he prioritised listening before talking, allowing for ideas to be actively discussed and exchanged. Stand-up meetings are what they are called in Bajaj Allianz—meetings that last long enough to complete while standing.

Karmayoga at work goes beyond just doing your duties. At a corporate level, it involves giving one's 100 per cent with a clear mind, without attaching emotions to decision-making and ethically following guidelines. That is the modern edition of the Karmayoga narrated in the Bhagawad Gita. Just like an artist can get immersed in one's work, mindfulness at work can be achieved by any patron.

Additionally, problem solving lies at the heart of Bajaj's growth. While the company is a profitable business, the motivation is to solve problems and to impact society at large by creating millions of jobs. When job creation and problem solving lie at the core of business growth, profitability is bound to follow.

'If somebody is in trouble, I feel it is my duty to be of assistance to them,' Tapan recollected on his empathetic leadership style. Compassion is such a core value that Tapan has even bent the HR rules at times to support his people when in time of need. Another value he exemplified was trust—entrusting his people has been a game changer in ensuring autonomous decision-making, innovative thinking and team work.

Being in the business of insurance leaves no room for lies and misrepresentation because Bajaj Allianz sells promises. Personal ethics and values have to be a notch higher than those in other industries. Therefore, hiring and firing are also done with core values and compassion at heart. Those employees who needed to be let go met Tapan personally and were coached on development areas and given some time to change and improve.

If improvements were not noticed, the employee was asked to move on only when he found another job. On the other hand, those with integrity issues, such as fraud or sexual harassment, were immediately asked to go. 'No one knows whom I have fired,' confirmed Tapan. 'Except for the one fired and me.'

Compassion also extended beyond the boardroom. When it came to managing difficult relationships and conversations at home, Tapan encouraged us to think, 'We are so polite to people we don't know, so why not with the ones we love?'

Food for thought for your next board meeting or family dinner.

Bibliography

Agteren, Joep van, Matthew Iasiello, Laura Lo, Jonathan Bartholomaeus, Zoe Kopsaftis, Marissa Carey and Michael Kyrios 'A Systematic Review and Meta-analysis of Psychological Interventions to Improve Mental Well-being'. *Nat Hum Behav* 5, 2021, pp. 631–52. https://doi.org/10.1038/s41562-021-01093-w

Andreychik, M. R. 'I Like That You Feel My Pain, but I Love That You Feel My Joy: Empathy For a Partner's Negative Versus Positive Emotions Independently Affect Relationship Quality. *Journal of Social and Personal Relationships*, 36(3), 2019, pp. 834–854. https://doi.org/10.1177/0265407517746518

Aronson, H. *Buddhist Practice on Western Ground: Reconciling Eastern Ideals and Western Psychology*. Shambhala (first edition): 2004.

Barad, J. 'The Understanding and Experience of Compassion: Aquinas and the Dalai Lama.' *Buddhist-Christian Studies*, 27, 2007, pp. 11–29. http://www.jstor.org/stable/30152891

Batchler, S. *After Buddhism – Rethinking the Dharma for a Secular Age*. Yale University Press: 2016.

Bhiku Bodhi. (1999). *The Noble Eightfold Path, Chapter 4, 'Right Action and Right Livelihood*'. https://www.accesstoinsight.org/lib/authors/bodhi/waytoend.html#ch4

Bhante Guanaratna. *Eight Mindful Steps to Happiness: Walking the Buddha's Path,* Wisdom Publications: 2001.

——. *Mindfulness in Plain English.* Wisdom Publications (20th anniversary edition): 2011.

Blackenhorn, D. 'How My View on Gay Marriage Changed'. *New York Times*, Opinion. 22 June 2012. https://www.nytimes.com/2012/06/23/opinion/how-my-view-on-gay-marriage-changed.html?smid=url-share

Bretherton, I. 'The Origins of Attachment Theory: John Bowlby and Mary Ainsworth'. *Developmental Psychology*, 28(5), 1992, pp. 759–75. https://doi.org/10.1037/0012-1649.28.5.759

Britannica. Editors of Encyclopedia (21 July 2017). 'Ashrama'. *Encyclopedia Britannica.* https://www.britannica.com/topic/ashrama

Brown, B. *Rising Strong: How the Ability to Reset Transforms the Way We Live, Love, Parent, and Lead.* Random House (reprint edition): 2017.

Chodron, Pema. *Wisdom of No Escape: And the Path of Loving Kindness.* Element Publishing: 2004.

——.'The Answer to Anger and Aggression is Patience.' *Lions Roar Magazine.* 16 November 2020. https://www.lionsroar.com/the-answer-to-anger-aggression-is-patience/

Conglton, C., Britta K. Holzel and Sarah W. Lazar. 'Mindfulness Can Literally Change Your Brain'. *Harvard Business Review,* 8 January 2015, pp. 2–5.

Dalai Lama. *The Power of Compassion.* Thorsons: 1995.

——. 'Compassion as the Source of Happiness'. https://www.dalailama.com/messages/compassion-and-human-values/compassion-as-the-source-of-happiness

Deccan Herald. 'Dalai Lama Says "bin Laden Killing Justified "'. 5 May 2011. https://www.deccanherald.com/content/159071/dalai-lama-says-bin-laden.html

DiChristina, M. 'Does Mindfulness Work?' *Scientific American (MIND)*, 2017, 7 December. https://www.scientificamerican.com/article/mindfulness-does-it-work/

Epstein, M. *Thoughts Without Thinker: Psychotherapy from a Buddhist Perspective*. Basic Books (revised edition): 2013.

Flaherty, S. C. and L. S. Sadler. 'A Review of Attachment Theory in the Context of Adolescent Parenting'. *Journal of Pediatric Health Care*, 25(2), 2011, pp. 114–21. https://doi.org/10.1016/j.pedhc.2010.02.005

Frankle, Viktor. *Man's Search for Meaning*. Beacon Press: first edition: 2006.

Fredrickson, B. L., M. A. Cohn, K. A. Coffey, J. Pek and S. M. Finkel. 'Open Hearts Build Lives: Positive Emotions, Induced through Loving-kindness Meditation, Build Consequential Personal Resources'. *Journal of Personality and Social Psychology*, 95(5), 2008, pp. 1045–62. https://doi.org/10.1037/a0013262

Goleman, D. and R. Davidson, R. *The Science of Meditation. How to Change Your Brain, Mind, and Body* (2nd ed). Penguin UK: 2017.

Germer, Chris. *The Mindful Path to Self-Compassion: Freeing Yourself from Destructive Thoughts and Emotions.* The Guilford Press (first edition): 2009.

——. (2019). 'Shame and the Wish to be Loved. Center for Mindful Self-Compassion'. 29 January 2019. https://centerformsc.org/shame-and-the-wish-to-be-loved/

Isaacson, Walter. *Steve Jobs*. Simon & Schuster (first edition): 2011.

Hart, William. *Art of Living* (first edition). HarperOne: (2009).

Harari, Y. *Sapiens: A Brief History of Humankind*. Harper (reprint edition): 2015.

Hölzel, B. K., J. Carmody, M. Vangel, C. Congleton, S. M. Yerramsetti, T. Gard and S. W. Lazar. 'Mindfulness Practice Leads to Increases in Regional Brain Gray Matter Density.' *Psychiatry Research*, 191(1), 36–43. https://doi.org/10.1016/j.pscychresns.2010.08.006

Hougaard, R., J. Carter. 'The Mind of a Leader'. *Harvard Business Review*, 13 March 2018.

Indursky, M. 'In Search of Happiness'. *Huffpost*, 3 June 2012, updated on 6 December 2017.

Kabat Zinn, Jon. *Full Catastrophe Living*. Little, Brown Book Group: 2013.

Killingsworth, M. A. and D. T. Gilbert. 'A Wandering Mind is an Unhappy Mind.' *Science*, 330(6006), 2010, p. 932. https://doi.org/10.1126/science.1192439

Kini, P. 'A Ferocious Voice for the Voiceless.' YahooNews, 18 December 2020.

Kulze, L. 'How Meditation Works.' *The Atlantic*, 27 June 2013, https://www.theatlantic.com/health/archive/2013/06/how-meditation-works/277275/

Landsberg, Mitchell. 'Dalai Lama Suggests bin Laden's Death Was Justified'. *Los Angeles Times*, 4 May 2011. https://www.latimes.com/local/la-xpm-2011-may-04-la-me-0504-dalai-lama-20110504-story.html

Lazar, S. 'Mindfulness Research'. *Mindfulness and Psychotherapy*, 22(11), 2005, pp. 220-38, https://www.anagrama.co.il/wp-content/uploads/2020/03/Mindfulness_and_Psychotherapy.pdf#page=238

Maslow, A. H. *Motivation and Personality*. Harper and Row: 1954.

——. *Motivation and Personality.* Pearson Education (third edition): 1987.

McGehee, P., C. Germer and K. D. Neff (2017). 'Core Values in Mindful Self-Compassion'. In L.M. Monteiro, R. F. Musten and J. C. Compson (eds), *A Practitioner's Guide to Mindfulness and Ethics*, pp. 279–294. New York: 2017. https://self-compassion.org/wp-content/uploads/2019/09/McGehee2017.pdf

McLeod, Saul. 'Maslow's Hierarchy of Needs', *Simply Psychology*, 2007. Retrieved from https://www.simplypsychology.org/maslow.html

——. 'Erik Erikson : Psychosocial Stages', *Simply Psychology.* 2008. Updated 25 January 2024. Retrieved from http://www.simplypsychology.org /Erik-Erikson.html

Mongrain, Myriam, Jacqueline Chin and Leah Shapira. 'Practicing Compassion Increases Happiness and Self-Esteem', *Journal of Happiness Studies*, 12 (201), pp. 963–81. 10.1007/s10902-010-9239-1.

Neff, Kristin. *Self-Compassion: The Proven Power of Being Kind to Yourself.* William Morrow Paperbacks (reprint edition): 2012.

Purser, R. *McMindfulness: How Mindfulness Became the New Capitalist Spirituality*. Repeater Books: 2019.

https://buddhistanarchism.files.wordpress.com/2020/04/mcmindfulness-ronald-purser.pdf

Radhakrishnan, S. *Bhagavadgita*. HarperCollins (new edition): 2011.

Raghunathan, R. *If You're So Smart, Why Aren't You Happy*? Portfolio (illustrated edition): 2016.

Ram Dass. *Be Here Now*. Harmony Publications: 1971.

Salzburg, Sharon. *Loving-kindness: The Revolutionary Art of Happiness.* Shambhala Publications: 2002.

Seligman, M. *Flourish*. Atria Books (reprint edition): 2012.

Staff of Psychology Today. 'Jealousy'. Reviewed by the Staff of Psychology Today. https://www.psychologytoday.com/us/basics/jealousy

Strauss, Clara Strauss, Billie Lever Taylor, Jenny Gu, Willem Kuyken, Ruth Baer, Fergal Jones, Kate Cavanagh. 'What is Compassion and How Can We Measure it? A Review of Definitions and Measures'. Clinical Psychology Review, 47, July 2016, pp. 15–27.

Swami Muktananda. 'Song of God'. https://www.holybhagavad-gita.org/chapter/3/verse/35

Tolle, E. *Power of Now*. New World Library: 1999.

Trungpa, Chogyam. *Cutting through Spiritual Materialism.* Shambala Publications: 1973.

Upadhyaya, K. 'The Impact of Early Buddhism on Hindu Thought (With Special Reference to the Bhagavadgītā)'. *Philosophy East and West,* 18(3), 1968, pp. 163-73.

Van Dam, N. T., M. K.van Vugt, D. R. Vago, L. Schmalzl, C. D. Saron, A. Olendzki, T. Meissner, S. W. Lazar, C. E. Kerr, J. Gorchov, K. Fox, B. A. Field, W. B. Britton, J. A. Brefczynski-Lewis and D. E. Meyer. 'Mind the Hype: A Critical Evaluation and Prescriptive Agenda for Research on Mindfulness and Meditation.' *Perspectives on Psychological Science: A Journal of the Association for Psychological Science,* 13(1), 2018, pp. 36–61. https://doi.org/10.1177/1745691617709589

Widgery, Alban G. 'The Principles of Hindu Ethics'. *International Journal of Ethics,* 40 (2), January 1930, pp. 232–45.

Winfrey, Graham. '4 Leadership Strategies Marc Benioff Swears By'. Inc.com, 18 June 2018. https://www.inc.com/graham-winfrey/marc-benioff-salesforce-ceo-leadership-lessons-facebook.html

Wiss, D. A., N. Avena and P. Rada. 'Sugar Addiction: From Evolution to Revolution'. *Frontiers in Psychiatry,* 9, 2018, p. 545. https://doi.org/10.3389/fpsyt.2018.00545

Websites

Excerpts from Steve Jobs biography: https://www.bookreporter.com/reviews/steve-jobs/excerpt

https://www.cnbc.com/2019/11/05/salesforce-ceo-marc-benioff-why-we-have-mindfulness-zones.html

https://jayshettygenius.com/blog/why-detached-love-is-infinite-and-pure-love/

Acknowledgements

'Within you, there is a stillness and sanctuary to which you can retreat at any time and be yourself.' —Hermann Hesse

Get Mindfulness Right was a book mysteriously hidden in the sanctuary of our fates. It took a little bit of convincing and retrospection to understand that we make a great team as co-authors. So, our first thank you is to each other: for bringing out the best in ourselves, for pushing our creative boundaries and for never losing momentum. And a big thank you to Professor Bhagwan Chowdhry for introducing us and kick-starting this book's journey.

Thank you Suhail Mathur (The Book Bakers), our literary agent, for representing this labour of love and swiftly bringing it to the hands of the right publisher. Your optimism and zeal is contagious and we can't thank you enough!

It has been a dream to get people to appreciate the practicality of mindfulness and we are grateful to Om Books International for giving us the platform to do so. A special thanks to our editor Jyotsna Mehta for enhancing the text with her insightful inputs.

Heartfelt gratitude to Dr Kiran Bedi, Shonali Bose, Dr Krishnamurthy Subramanian, Dr Raj Raghunathan and

Tapan Singhel, for taking time out of their busy schedules and entertaining two curious women who probed about their trysts with mindfulness. Your wisdom has been invaluable to this book.

My (Swati) philosophical interest in all things spiritual began with my mother Vibha who taught me to logically examine traditions before practising them. My husband, Bhagwan, a professor who finds evidence as a necessary component for believing in a phenomenon, watered and nourished the seeds that were planted by my mother. He has been my biggest support in my two-decade-long mindfulness journey. My children, Paheli and Saransh, are my biggest teachers and truly inspire me to be mindful of my own patterns that do not fit into our world. I am so fortunate to have the trust and support from all my siblings and from Bhagwan's family. The works of my Eastern and Western teachers, His Holiness the Dalai Lama, Guru Goenkaji, Joseph Goldstein, Mark Epstein, Richard Davidson and Jack Kornfield, have influenced me tremendously. I am forever grateful for their lifetime dedication to the practice and teachings around mindfulness. I am indebted to my teachers at vipassana centres in India and Spirit Rock Meditation Center in California. Above all this, I need to mention four tremendous teachers who have not only taught me but are also personal friends: Trudy Goodman, Chris Germer, Chris Chapple and Beth Sternlieb. I am inspired by their life journey.

Lastly, I am immensely grateful to all my students of mindfulness and compassion whose questions not only add to my knowledge of mindfulness, but also make me feel so humbled when I see them evolving with ease by diligently practising the teachings.

My (Subhashini) journey with mindfulness has just begun and I have to thank my immediate family who have contributed to it: Amma and Appa, for being the most compassionate individuals I know. Aravind, my brother, for having the most rock-solid core values. Ayush, for being an equal partner and playing the role as a parent with non-attachment. And to Arhaan and Aarna, my children, for teaching me the art of living in the present moment every single day. And to my first meditation teacher, Kshama Desai, for planting the first seeds of mindfulness. To all my family, maternal, paternal and in-laws for encouraging me to write.

Last but never the least, to the readers who have picked this book up with hope, thank you. May your mindfulness journey be fulfilling.